"If the wisdom and advice
book – based on robust d... ... . — ....
up by couples, so much of the heartbreak and pain
experienced by adults and children in our society may
be avoided."

Nicky and Sila Lee, Founders of The Marriage Course

"A life-changing read for anyone looking for reliable
love! This compact book is full of wisdom based on
robust research and real-life experiences. It has the
potential to redirect the course of couple relationships
away from ambiguity and into committed, successful
marriages in a modern era."

**Michaela Hyde, Executive Director, Marriage
Foundation**

"*Commit or Quit* is a response to the rise in
committed, or not so committed couple relationships,
providing a framework for people to appreciate their
choices."

**Richard and Maria Kane, Marriage Week International,
Marriage-week.org**

"Ever the curator of up-to-date information on today's
relationships, Harry synthesizes current research and
theory to offer practical, contemporary advice for
those in modern relationships. This book is a must-
read for anyone living together."

**Prof Galena Rhoades, Center for Marital and
Family Studies, University of Denver**

"All too many couples drift into cohabitation without a plan or a clear sense of their future. This is a mistake, as couples who drift into cohabitation and then marriage are much more likely to end up unhappy and divorced. *Commit or Quit* offers a better path for men and women whose ultimate aim is a stable and happy marriage. Cohabiting men and women who would like to marry should definitely read this book."

Bradford Wilcox, Director, National Marriage Project Professor, Department of Sociology, University of Virginia

"*Commit or Quit* comes with a simple message to all couples to have a 'forever conversation'. This is delivered alongside an avalanche of evidence from Harry Benson who sets out why the intentionality around marriage makes a difference to the likely longevity of a relationship.

This isn't just a relationship self-help guide – although every young man should read it – this book has implications for governments too. The more we strengthen couple relationships the less family breakdown and human misery we will see around us. This book outlines how couples who decide to commit to sticking together are more likely to do so than those who simply slide into an ever more constrained relationship. The evidence is clearly and succinctly put in another great book by Harry Benson."

Frank Young, Head of Family Policy, Centre for Social Justice

COMMIT OR QUIT

The Two-Year Rule and Other Rules for Romance

HARRY BENSON

LION

Published by
Lion Hudson Limited
Wilkinson House, Jordan Hill Business Park
Banbury Road, Oxford OX2 8DR, England
www.lionhudson.com

ISBN 978 0 7459 8080 5
eISBN 978 0 7459 8081 2

First edition 2020

Acknowledgments
Unless otherise indicated, scripture quotations taken from the *Holy Bible,
New International Version*, copyright © 1973, 1978, 1984 International Bible
Society. Used by permission of Hodder & Stoughton, a member of the Hodder
Headline Group. All rights reserved. "NIV" is a trademark of International
Bible Society. UK trademark number 1448790.

Scripture quotation marked ESV is from The Holy Bible, English Standard
Version® (ESV®) copyright © 2001 by Crossway, a publishing ministry of Good
News Publishers. All rights reserved.

A catalogue record for this book is available from the British Library

Printed and bound in the UK, April 2020, LH26

To all those who are stuck.
May you be blessed with the wisdom
and courage to know whether you need
either to commit or to quit.

CONTENTS

> *Lauren was eyeing up wedding rings. Lee was eyeing up somebody else.*

> *Birth control has changed the game of relationships over the last fifty years. But we are not playing it very well.*

> *Time and time again I hear stories of women living in what should be a perfectly good relationship but which is going nowhere. Stuck.*

> *All of us want reliable love. We need somebody to whom we can commit and who will commit to us. But what does commitment mean?*

> *Some good things in life happen by accident. Most happen because somebody made a plan. Why should relationships be any different?*

> *An essential ingredient of any successful relationship is the resolution of any lingering anxiety and ambiguity. What we all need is clarity.*

*You'd choose a business partner with great care. And
so it should be with a life partner. Here are two simple
rules that will help you choose well.*

*What puts a marriage at risk in the early years is not a
lack of love. It's the way we treat each other badly. Here
are four STOP signs to watch out for.*

*The odds are stacked in your favour if you marry – and
against if you don't – because marriage has all the
ingredients needed to make a relationship work.*

*It's easy for a relationship to drift without a plan or
clear intentions. Is there a right time to have that
conversation? Yes. It's the two-year rule.*

*We've lost confidence in our ability to give wise advice
to younger couples who are drifting. But that's exactly
what they need and want.*

All the references and a bit more detail for the studies cited in
this book.

FOREWORD

Back in the day, which for the purposes of these short remarks I shall define as pre-1970, everyone knew, and implicitly consented to, the basic rules or conventions that governed the structure and ordering of family life. And these rules applied whether you were born into life in a castle or a council house (local authority public housing). Put simply, you were generally born into a family consisting of a mother, a father, and 2.4 children. And when your turn came, you found, by one means or other, a partner for yourself. If and when the relationship developed you too would become engaged, marry, and then, and only then, have children. This basic family progression was underpinned and reinforced by three taboos. The taboos were:

- there was no sexual intercourse, and certainly no children born, before marriage
- no couple cohabited if they were unmarried
- divorce was not acceptable.

Of course, these taboos were often honoured more in the breach than in the observance but any such breach risked serious social stigma by your elders and peers. And this set of rules and taboos had been the norm for society for literally hundreds of years. I clearly remember my father, an otherwise mild-mannered man, instilling fear into my sisters with regards to the dire consequences that would flow from non-observance. His position was universally held and non-negotiable.

The intended or unintended consequence of this agreed pattern was that testosterone-driven young men, eager to taste the full sexual delights of their girlfriends, focused in short order on whether she would qualify as his life-time partner and spouse and whether a proposal of marriage should follow. Similarly, girls tended to snap up the offers of marriage when they arose. The macro effects of this abundance of unfulfilled sexual desire was that couples mostly made up their minds quickly, married in their early twenties, and had children shortly after. Almost no one "lived in sin", as cohabiting was then rather quaintly described.

However, within a few short years of 1970, and the coincidental arrival of the contraceptive pill, these age-old rules, conventions, and taboos had evaporated. Sex before marriage, illegitimate birth, and indeed divorce, quickly became acceptable norms for all – from the Royal family downwards. There is not the space here and nor is it the place to discuss the detailed reasons for these truly unexpected changes of human behaviour, suffice it to say that the effect on the coupling process of young people was unpredicted, far-reaching, and profound. It was a bit like tearing up the Highway Code (rules of the road) and allowing drivers to make their own choices about, for example, which side of the road they would like to drive on. Inevitably traffic anarchy ensues.

It is perhaps a cliché, but nevertheless a true one, that a complete social and sexual revolution has occurred in the last few decades and during that time we have largely been making it up as we go along, unhindered by any of the old norms. Fortunately, however, not everyone has been asleep at the wheel. As a result of a great deal of high-grade research in the UK, and especially in the US, we have come a long way in our understanding of the causes and effects of these speedy and dramatic changes in human behaviour. We are now able to understand and make sense of the enigma and complexities of "commitment" and especially the very different commitment process followed by men as opposed to women

The simple statistical effect of these changes is that in the UK now there are 3 million couples who cohabit unmarried.[1]

On the outside these couples exhibit many of the features of a married couple: they live together, share their lives together, and have children. However, on the inside, the psychological difference is fundamental, especially so far as women are concerned. Women in particular (but sometimes men too) frequently find themselves stuck in a limbo situation not knowing whether their partner is in it for the long term or merely hanging on for want of anything better and planning to leave at a moment's notice, unhindered by any legal or other constraints. And although many of these cohabiting relationships are successful, statistically speaking, they are three times more likely to break up than married couples. We all know of such couples. Many women will be thinking of whether to start planning a family, but for older women time might not be on their side. Women are invariably the biggest losers.

Now this clever book is the first serious analysis of this commonly occurring limbo status: how it happens, why it happens and, crucially, how long one or other of the couple should endure it before they pull the plug. In other words, the author proposes some new "rules" to replace the old and suggests that both young people of both sexes, and their sometimes bewildered parents, should understand and absorb them. Doing so will enable them to navigate, without harm, life's now churned-up social waters and so make the right choices.

I have worked closely with Harry Benson (as research director of Marriage Foundation) for many years now. He knows, inside out, all the current national and international (mostly American) research that is out there. He is steeped in it. Indeed, much of it he has carried out himself either on his own or with other English and foreign academics. His great gift is his ability to make this seemingly dry research highly accessible and enjoyable reading. And ultimately truly fascinating. Additionally, he has folded into the research personal experience on the ground (via his family: wife and six children) and his wide circle of friends.

The traditional taboos, stigmas, and norms have long gone. The social and sexual Highway Code has been consigned to the fire. And I, for one, would rejoice and say good riddance to their departure, causing so much human misery as they often did. However, dispensing with the old rules as we have, young people forging long-term and fully sexualized relationships at, say, university – or beyond – are entitled to and need good research-based advice and information, not anecdote and moralizing, to enable them to appreciate fully what they are doing and to ensure that they are making good choices.

This book is the new traffic manual. Essential reading for those in their late teens, twenties, and thirties... and their parents!

But also, for all of us trying to make sense of society's contemporary self-management style, now operating without rules, this slim volume enables us at last to peer through the fog and make our own informed judgments.

Sir Paul Coleridge
Chairman and founder of Marriage Foundation
September 2019

ACKNOWLEDGMENTS

Two people, more than any other, have inspired my work in championing marriage and commitment: the brilliant American social scientist professors – Scott Stanley and Galena Rhoades – at the University of Denver. I have known them for at least a decade now. They're not just world leaders in the field of commitment research; they're also exceptionally nice people. I hope they reap the rewards in full for their years of groundbreaking work in helping so many people understand why marriage and cohabitation are simply not the same thing. I really am grateful to them.

I am also hugely grateful to my friend and colleague at Marriage Foundation – Sir Paul Coleridge. He has given me a high-profile public platform from which to research, write, and talk about marriage, cohabitation, and commitment. The fact that he was a senior judge in the family division of the High Court has given our work added gravitas and helped us achieve over 1,000 pieces of significant media coverage in just seven years. This is the second foreword he has written for me and I really appreciate both his support and his encouragement.

Thanks also to Professor Steve McKay at the University of Lincoln. We have worked together on and off for over fifteen years now. He is one of these extraordinary understated and unsung academics of brilliance and integrity who honours whatever findings he gets from his analyses, even when the results sometimes take us by surprise. In response, I have always been very careful to stick to what he tells me the data allow us to conclude and not try to make claims that aren't justified. He won't tell anyone, but he is effectively world stats champion, having won the Stanford statistics challenge in the US fairly recently. It is my privilege to work with him.

Our stats are quoted by politicians and journalists and I sometimes get credited with these. Each of our papers starts with an idea. But without Steve's ability to construct the complex analyses that test these ideas, our findings would never have seen the light of day.

Of course, it's no good producing fancy research with insightful findings if you don't get them out into the public domain. For most of our time at Marriage Foundation, we've been advised on all things media by Beatrice Timpson at MIPPR (Media Intelligence Partners). She has now moved on to different pastures but she's been a rock for us and to her I'm really grateful. Some of the key ideas in this book came from Beatrice.

I'm also enormously grateful to the team at Lion Hudson, who have been through a testing time. Thank you to Jon Oliver for commissioning the book, Lyn Roberts for getting it to press, Miranda Lever for editing the flow of the book, and to my former editor Tony Collins who has always been a big fan of the idea behind this book. A big thank you also to Rhoda Hardie who did such an amazing job publicizing my last book that we took her on at Marriage Foundation. She's helped with the publicity for this book too. She's one of the most polite and kind people I know. No wonder journalists warm to her.

And a special thank you to my amazing family. As well as being CEO of the Benson household, Kate is my rock, lover, and best friend. We made a promise over thirty years ago and are living out its benefits. Note that well as you read this book! Our future is brighter than ever, especially now that our six children have nearly all left home. Talking of which, I'm so grateful to my brilliant Rosie, Polly, Grace, Sizzle, Charlie, and Johnnie for allowing me to test my ideas on them. They are proof that children do sometimes actually listen and apply their parents' suggestions. My "rules for romance" have been road-tested by them!

ACKNOWLEDGMENTS

And finally, I may work in the secular realm with the very best research and evidence. But I am also proud to say that I was lost and now am found. I couldn't do any of this without Jesus. Thank you.

THEIR FUTURE: IN HER HEAD

Lauren had just caught the bouquet at her best friend's wedding when she saw the text that gave it away.

She had been wondering hopefully if Lee might take the opportunity to pop the question tonight. The setting of their hotel was idyllic. She could picture him making a charmingly clumsy speech with a big grin on his face.

The phone he had left on the table lit up with a text. She picked it up.

The message was from Liz, an old friend of hers from primary school. It seemed odd really because she and Lee didn't know each other. She'd introduced them at a reunion a few months ago, but that was it.

In her message, Liz said she'd booked them the hotel in Croatia for the weekend.

That was doubly strange because Lee had told her he had to go to a work weekend in Glasgow. He'd been really apologetic, weirdly apologetic in fact, given that he (seemingly) had no choice...

When Lauren met Lee six years earlier at that party, she had heard about his reputation as a philanderer. But he seemed so smitten with her. His face would light up when she entered the room. Maybe she was the one to tame him.

And for six years he had been all hers. Or so she had thought.

They'd had a great time together. Six years she had given him. She'd assumed he was as committed to her as she was to him.

But the longer they'd spent together, the more she'd closed her eyes to the little warning signs. He only ever talked about their future in the vaguest of terms. On the rare occasions the conversation came round to marriage, his answers were evasive yet gave her just enough to keep her hopes and dreams alive.

Of course, one day. Don't worry. Trust me. I love you.

With every year that they lived together, it seemed like Lee was going to be it, the one. And so she'd pushed any lingering doubts and uncertainties about their relationship to the back of her mind. The prospect of starting all over again at age thirty-two was not appealing. She would make it work whatever.

So, without realizing it, she found herself stuck in a relationship where she was never completely sure what he felt or how strongly. She had grown afraid to ask.

Now it made sense.

She was the one who'd planned their future. She was the one who was committed. They would get married, have children. They would grow old together. She would make sure he was never lonely, and he would do the same for her.

But Lauren had been wrong. Totally and utterly wrong. She was eyeing up wedding rings. Lee was eyeing up somebody else.

Their future was all in her head. It just wasn't in his.

ALL CHANGE IN THE GAME OF LOVE

Attitudes to sex, relationships, and marriage have changed enormously over the last fifty years.

We have undergone a sexual revolution. Society is less stuffy, less rigid, and less patriarchal. There is more individual choice, freedom, and sex.

It has been an unmitigated improvement to human development, hasn't it? Well, there's a problem.

Birth control may have changed the game. But we are not yet playing it very well.

Women may have been liberated from the risk of pregnancy. But so too have men been liberated from the need to commit.

The result is unreliable love.

The new phenomenon of cohabitation

Living together seems such a sensible idea. But it is not risk-free.

For some it will turn out to be a precursor or alternative to marriage. But for many others it is an arrangement fraught with assumptions, ambiguity, and asymmetric commitment that traps couples – like Lauren and Lee – and ultimately wrecks hopes and dreams.

For my parents', grandparents', and previous generations, when boy met girl and they liked each other, it was generally up to the boy to do all of the running. Not only would he have to prove himself worthy to her, he would have to prove himself worthy to her parents. After an appropriate length of time, he would ask her father for permission to marry his daughter. Only after permission was secured could he get down on one knee and propose marriage. Once married – and only once married – could they be free to live together, have sex together, and have children together.

Up until the 1970s, it was considered taboo to have sex as an unmarried couple. Quite simply sex carried with it too big a risk of pregnancy. Obviously it happened. But sex outside marriage was rare and furtive.[1]

Moving in together as an unmarried couple was out of the question. Almost all couples got married before they slept together, let alone moved in together. Or if they did sleep together and it led to pregnancy, couples generally did the "right thing" and got married in a "shotgun" wedding – the expression being derived from the groom being forced to the altar at the end of the barrel of a shotgun held by the girl's father. Marriage almost always preceded parenthood.[2]

The advent of the female contraceptive pill changed everything.

Although physical contraceptives have been around since the 1900s, it wasn't until the 1960s that the oral pill became available for married women and the 1970s that it also became available for unmarried women. What the pill did was allow couples to sleep together, and even cohabit together, without fear of pregnancy. It liberated both men and women.

When my wife-to-be Kate and I began to go out together in the 1980s, we were among the first generation of young unmarried adults to take advantage of this new freedom.

But even if sleeping together as an unmarried couple no longer carried the risk of pregnancy, it was still frowned upon socially. I well remember visiting friends for the weekend and being placed firmly in separate rooms by the host parents.

"Corridor creeping" was the only way to enjoy each other's company while not causing offence.

When we moved in together formally, it was only accepted by our parents' generation because we were going to get married a month later and were buying a flat as our marital home. And, of course, I had made sure to ask Kate's father's permission to marry his daughter before I got down on one knee and asked Kate herself.

Social behaviour may have changed. But social norms take a little while longer to catch up.

Today, few couples now worry about holding off from having sex until they get married. Sex is an integrated and expected part of the courting process. The main question is whether sex happens on the first, second, or third date.

Moving in together has also become fully normalized and socially accepted, so much so that marriage has become optional. Today, only half of parents are married at the time of their baby's birth. Only two thirds of parents will have married each other before their child leaves school.[3]

Until the pill arrived on the scene, the link between commitment, marriage, living together, sex, and children had been pretty clear throughout recent human history. There was a strict order in which things happened in a relationship.

After the arrival of the pill, those links have been well and truly broken. The order of things is now far more flexible. Sex invariably comes first, usually followed by living together and children. And whereas commitment used to involve a clear public statement that was linked to marriage, now it can mean whatever a couple chooses it to mean.

As the popularity of unmarried cohabitation has ballooned and the popularity of marriage has retreated, so family breakdown has reached record levels that are almost certainly the highest in history.

This doesn't just matter because ambiguous relationships leave behind a trail of heartbroken adults. It matters because there are often children involved. Today at least a third of all sixteen-year-olds in the UK are not living with both natural parents.[4] And family breakdown is the number one driver of mental health difficulties among teenagers.[5]

I should be clear that this passes no judgment on lone parents, few of whom are on their own by choice. Lone parents do a remarkable job with one pair of hands and most of their children do perfectly well in life.

But just because human beings can cope with fewer resources and can prove remarkably resilient in all sorts of circumstances, it doesn't mean we should just sit back and accept that it's OK.

We can do better – a lot better.

Same old human nature

We may have changed the way we form relationships. But our underlying human nature, the way relationships work, has not changed.

- All of us still want the same kind of reliable love that lasts.
- All of us still need time to work out whether a fledgling relationship has the potential to provide that kind of love.
- All of us still need to be free to walk away if we learn that it doesn't have that potential.
- And when we have learned enough about one another, all of us still need to make some kind of mutual commitment to one another that gives us real clarity, confidence, and security in a future together and that removes any lingering doubts or ambiguity.

Like it or not, the genie is out of the bottle. Birth control is here to stay and cannot be disinvented. Cohabitation is the new norm. Marriage is optional.

Understanding how to give couples who cohabit a better chance of staying together, and therefore making their life all it could and should be, is the point of this book.

What's in the book

In **chapter 1** I will introduce you to some couples whose stories illustrate powerfully how not to make a relationship work.

I have changed names and camouflaged some of the details to retain their anonymity. But these are real people. I hope you will be able to relate to their stories, whether through your own experience of relationships or that of somebody you know.

For me, most of the clues for how to get it wrong – despite good intentions – can be found in these stories. In fact, when I was first planning to write this book, these were the people I had in mind. Each of them has generously told me things in confidence that are usually very private. I hope I have done them justice.

Chapters 2 and **3** explain what's going on in our relationships by looking at what commitment is really all about.

Here I am enormously grateful to my friends Professors Scott Stanley and Galena Rhoades at the University of Denver in the USA. Their work on commitment, both theoretical and practical, has helped me understand relationships better than I ever did beforehand.

When I describe their concepts of "dedication" and "constraints" to you, I think you will get it. And when I tell you about "sliding or deciding" in relationships, I know you will get it.

Just to be sure, I've included more stories of real people and some analogies that will help you visualize what's going on.

Real relationships always start with a dance, where each partner tries to figure out what their own intentions are and also those of their partner. So in **chapter 4** I'll talk about ambiguity and asymmetry in relationships.

Ambiguity means the lingering uncertainty about where things are going. And asymmetry is where one person is less committed than the other. More often than not, it's the man who holds the power to pull the plug.

In the end, commitment is about finding a way to bring clarity so that both of you know where you are. My marriage to Kate began with ambiguity and uncertainty when we were courting. Today, over thirty years into our married life, we have great certainty and equality about each other's commitment. How did that transition happen?

By the time you reach **chapter 5** you should have a really clear understanding of how relationships form and what makes them work. It's time to put some of this into practice so that we can help our next generation of young adults to choose well.

For the last decade or so, my six children have been emerging from their teenage years and on into adulthood. I have therefore had time for plenty of conversations about boyfriends and girlfriends along the way.

Using the research, and hopefully a bit of wisdom, I came up with a set of "rules for romance", two simple principles or guidelines for my kids to help them in their own search for reliable love.

I am delighted – and relieved – that they have applied these rules really well in their own lives, whether to pick a boyfriend or to break up with, or in one case so far to marry him.

So now I offer my two simple "rules for romance" to help you choose equally well!

Having chosen well, relating well is also pretty important. It's no good finding a really lovely person if we then don't treat them at all well. And yet all of us mistreat one another at some stage or another. We don't mean to, but it happens anyway when we react badly or get defensive or lash out at the one we love.

In **chapter 6** I will take you through four bad habits – what I call STOP signs – that undermine successful relationships and, most importantly, the messages from our past or upbringing that drive them.

All of us use one or more STOP signs. I'll tell you mine. I hope it will help you identify yours and help you change the message.

So we can choose well. We can treat each other with kindness and rewrite the negative messages that make us react badly to one another. But should we get married?

Of course, nobody has to get married. But, as I will discuss in **chapter 7**, the odds of a successful relationship and thriving family life are hugely stacked in your favour, and your children's favour, if you do.

My own research at Marriage Foundation shows that between seven and eight out of ten married parents manage to stay together while bringing up their children. Contrast this with the three out of ten unmarried parents who stay together.[6]

Yet it's clear that, as well as the majority of married parents, a minority of parents who don't marry do perfectly well. I'll talk about what I think is going on here and I won't beat about the bush with my conclusion: get married before you have children.

Is there an ideal time to get married? I think there is. Or at the very least, I think there is an ideal time to clear the air, make sure you're both on the same page, and make a commitment one way or another: to commit or quit.

In **chapter 8**, I reveal the results of some new analysis I did with my colleague Professor Steve McKay on what couples do after living together for a while. In essence, however long couples have lived together, their chances of splitting up remain much the same but their chances of getting married decline.

So waiting longer before getting married doesn't help your chances of finding reliable love but it does make your chances of getting married worse. And only one in ten couples will be happily unmarried and still together ten years on.

But after asking more than 300 people in another online survey, also especially for this book, it turns out I'm thinking along the same lines as most other people.

The vast majority think couples really ought to have had that conversation about where they are going with their lives by two years as an optimum and three years as a maximum. This is when couples really need to commit or quit.

Two years, whether living together or not, is more than enough time for most people to have found out what they need to know in order to decide whether this is the partnership that can go the distance.

And that is my "two-year rule".

But when you're talking to couples who have been drifting in their relationship, and may be a little stuck, how do you make this suggestion with suitable gentleness and compassion?

In **chapter 9**, I finish with some wonderful examples of parents I know who have done exactly this with their adult children. The consequences in both cases have been that uncertain relationships have been converted into marriage. Both relationships have benefited hugely because of the resulting clarity and security.

Commit or Quit

As you will see from the stories dotted throughout the book, it's all too easy for couples to drift on in their relationship without clarifying their plans for the future. Where there's a less committed partner, there may be no particular desire to clarify things. But for the more committed partner, there is a creeping fear of raising the subject.

Until this ambiguity is resolved, the relationship will always fall short of its potential. But having that conversation is exactly what needs to happen to prevent years of wasted drift.

My hope is that the "two-year rule" will become a widely used expression that parents and friends can wave around to break the aimless drift and encourage couples either to commit or quit.

But enough talking about what the book contains.

Time to commit to reading it!

CHAPTER 1

STUCK ON YOU

Time and time again I hear stories of women living in what should be a perfectly good relationship but which is going nowhere.

She and her partner have spent years together. In most cases – by no means all, as we shall see – she longs for him to ask her to marry him. Even if they aren't going to marry specifically, she needs clarity about their future together. She just wants to know the plan. Instead she has to put up with a state of ambiguity.

Of course, it's not always the man who struggles with the idea of commitment. But in two out of three cases, it is the man who is dragging his heels.

As the clock ticks relentlessly on, she is increasingly aware that if she wants to have children, her window of opportunity is narrowing. If it isn't to be with him, she needs to know. The thought of having to go through the process of finding somebody else is too exhausting to contemplate.

As things stand now, she doesn't have any good reason to leave him. She loves him and knows they could have a good life together.

But the whole subject of commitment and marriage has become ever more difficult to discuss. They might

> have talked and joked about it early on. But now it's become a no-go area.
>
> She's frustrated by the uncertainty. Yet she is scared of raising the subject.
>
> She's stuck.

Men eventually want to marry

It used to be that boys had to prove themselves in order to get the girl. The price of sex was commitment. No more.

Now it's all on a plate.

I remember watching a teen film with my daughters a few years ago, when I heard one of the older girls in the film warn one of the younger girls that it's no good giving away ice creams for nothing when what you really want them to do is to buy the whole store.[1]

Free sex goes a long way to explain why young men no longer see the need for commitment. Of course, this is not all young men. But the evidence points in this direction.

In one of several new studies I did especially for this book, based on a survey of 2,000 adults, I found that men in their late twenties were 33% *less* likely than women of the same age to say they wanted to get married at some stage. However, by the time they were in their thirties, men were slightly *more* likely than women to want to get married.[2]

This switch between the genders can also be seen among those who have an ideological objection to marriage.

Among the under thirties, men were more likely than women to say they are not married because they think either it's not necessary, or they've seen too many divorces, or they don't like the expectations or values surrounding marriage. However, among the over thirties, it's women who were more likely to have an ideological objection.

Perhaps surprisingly, the majority of ideological objectors

did not rule out marriage altogether for themselves. Although the numbers are small – less than one in six of all unmarried people – more men than women under thirty objected to marriage and ruled it out, whereas the balance was more even among the over thirties.

So when I say that younger men have a problem with commitment, I'm not talking about all men. I'm simply saying that if somebody in a relationship has a problem with commitment, more often than not it's the man.

Real stories about stuckness

I've also interviewed a number of people for this book, in order to illustrate and bring to life the principles that emerge from the kind of numbers I've just discussed.

All of my stories involve real people with real situations. I've changed their names and camouflaged some of the details to give them anonymity.

I hope you will connect with something in each story, so that it relates to somebody you know. Yes, that's him. Yes, that's her. Yes, that's me.

Some of the stories have a happy-ever-after feel about them, although all that really means is that the person in question is in a better place right now. Other stories are more open-ended and don't really have an ending.

I want to start with one of each of these.

To begin, Marie's story reflects the stereotype of a relationship that might have blossomed into something quite special but never quite gets there because her boyfriend Martin simply wouldn't commit. She holds out for the dream, living in hope that something magical would happen.

The trouble is that the longer the relationship goes on, the harder it becomes for either of them to commit or quit. It takes something fairly dramatic – marriage, pregnancy, an affair – to break the deadlock one way or another.

Until then, she is stuck.

After that, Anna's story reflects the less common – but still very real – situation of a woman who won't – or can't – commit.

She too is stuck.

Marie's story

In the beginning, Martin and I were really good together as a couple. Although we talked a lot about marriage and children early on, neither of these materialized. And the longer we stayed together the more we drifted apart. He wasn't unkind but he was selfish. He always put his career above me. Eventually, after seven years together, he just walked out. Our relationship had been drifting and he'd been having an affair. I don't know which came first. But the warning signs were there and I should have seen them. Did I waste seven years? You decide.

I met Martin when five of us shared a house together for our last year at university in the Midlands. I hadn't known him until then. But after just a few weeks of chatting over coffees and breakfasts, I fell in love and we moved into the same room. I loved his ideas, his values, and his ambition.

Because I felt this was a relationship that was going somewhere, we joked a lot about children and even came up with names.

After we both graduated, I still hadn't quite worked out what I wanted to do with my life. He had a job lined up in the City and so it seemed natural to follow him there.

However, talk of children proved premature. Stuck in London, I quickly realized I had put my own life on hold. I had subordinated my life to his and needed space. So I left him and headed back north to my family.

I did think of him from time to time during the next year. So when one day he rang to invite me down for a party, I accepted. We moved back in together more or less immediately.

Although we talked about marriage, we didn't do anything about it. Life in London was fun but I really wanted children and a clear statement of commitment.

Four years on, the subject of marriage came up in a conversation at my parents' house. They went into overdrive. I could sense Martin recoiling from the plans that instantly began to take shape. After that, we seriously discussed eloping.

Once again, nothing came of it. Over time, I even persuaded myself that I didn't need marriage. But I wanted children and I wanted commitment.

I was lucky enough to find a job as a school administrator near where we lived. But Martin worked long hours when he was in London and was often away seeing clients around the country.

One day he came back from work and announced, out of the blue, that he was leaving. He gave no reasons, although I knew we hadn't been getting on particularly well for the previous eighteen months or so. I asked him if he was having an affair. He swore blind that he wasn't.

So that was it. It was all over in a flash. Seven years together ended with no real explanation. I did find out a couple of weeks later that he had moved in with the work colleague with whom he had actually been having an affair.

I don't know what hurt more: his duplicity and deceit at cheating on me; his cold refusal to explain his sudden departure; or my own foolishness at not seeing the warning signs and leaving sooner.

What would the older me say to the younger me?

I shouldn't have been so quick to move in with him after our break. I should have waited until I'd seen some evidence that he put me first, rather than his career. In going back to him, I allowed his plans to dominate my own.

I also waited far too long for him to commit. When his warm words failed to turn into actions, I even persuaded myself that I didn't need – or even want – to get married. Most of all, I should have seen the light when he actively backed away from marriage.

I don't think all of those seven years were wasted. But I should have got out when I could have done so at twenty-five rather than waiting to be broken up with at age thirty.

Anna's story

David and I are in our late thirties. We have been living together for eight years and bought a house in joint names three years ago. Neither of us has much of a clearly expressed plan for the future. But I suppose we are happy enough together. We have two dogs and no children. So we've got all the paraphernalia of married life but without much of a plan to marry. I like today but have no idea what tomorrow will look like.

I think the problem is more with me.

In the first year that we were together, David talked about getting married. He definitely wanted to get married. But we haven't talked about it since.

I suppose we've committed in other ways. I mean, we've bought a house together. We've got dogs. So where would we go?

The question I always have is "Is this it?"

There are lots of pros. He's a great bloke, very amenable and easy going, which I value and recognize. He's good at building relationships. My family like him.

The main con is that I'm scared of making a decision. I'm better at living in the present, day to day, rather than future-oriented. I think he worries that if he ever did ask me, I might not say yes. So he's not so sure any more. The lack of a long-term plan causes him not to sleep. That's not good.

Although I'm nearly forty, motherhood doesn't have that pull on me that it seems to have on other women. I've never had maternal instincts. I like children and am perfectly good with them. But I have never experienced that desperate longing to have my own.

The longer we go on together, the further any decisions about our future – marriage, children – get pushed away.

On the one hand, I worry about missing out on being a mother and wonder who will look after me in my dotage. On the other, I fear that if we had children we might split up or I might not be a good parent.

So are we in the right relationship? Is it a mistake to stay? Would it be a bigger mistake to leave?

I just don't know. And so we stick with what we have, stuck.

My core problem is that I really don't like making decisions. I'm not good at committing to things that I can't get out of. I'm scared of them.

I've had counselling which wasn't very fruitful. I can talk about it and articulate it. But I haven't yet worked out why it's so hard to push me over the finish line in any decision.

My family background is bound to play a part. My parents are still together despite a huge blip in their marriage. Dad had a very complicated affair and, because he also worked away a lot, I didn't see him much during my teenage years. Mum is an extraordinary woman and somehow she was able to take him back. I envy their ability to finish each other's sentences. But they still bicker a lot and I don't like that.

I don't know if this is the way I am. But I do know I worry about making decisions, such as whether to stay here, whether to do this job. I know I have a good life. I like my work. I come home. I walk the dogs.

I just realized I didn't mention David. We get on fine and it's all fine. I just don't know if I'd be happier elsewhere.

If he did propose, I know it would change my outlook on life. It would give me more certainty and would definitely make me feel differently about our life together. But thinking about it now, I still think we'd struggle with the nitty gritty of everyday life.

I guess I'm a "glass half-empty" person. So we're stuck.

Stuck

It's tough reading these stories, isn't it?

In real life, Marie is now happily married. But as she talked through her story to me, it was very striking how quickly the hurt returned years after the event. Whether it was the waste of time with somebody who didn't care for her, or being cheated on behind her back, or then broken up with out of the blue, or probably being a little young and foolish in hanging around for so long, this stuff hurts.

Could she have done it differently? Had I been her father, I would have gently enquired whether she was happy to put her own life into second place behind his without a clear plan for their future. Marie might have realized a lot earlier that she was doing all the running and therefore Martin was falling short of one of my "rules for romance" that I talk about in chapter 5. He was not fighting for her.

I hope Marie would also have felt empowered by the "two-year rule" that I describe in chapter 8. So even if she had continued with him, she would also have been able to draw a line in the sand to stop the drift.

Who knows?

However, I find Anna's story more depressing because her being stuck seems to lack a solution. I'm not sure she would really want to marry David even if he were to ask. But as things stand, I would worry that either of them is vulnerable to a bit of kindness being shown by somebody else.

It seems to me that without a clear commitment, this relationship is an accident waiting to happen. It might last a few years but it's fundamentally unstable. It's not sustainable.

Somebody somewhere needs to help them get out of this state of "stuckness".

Both of them want and need reliable love. And they will only find that if they commit or quit.

So what does commitment look like?

CHAPTER 2

LOOKING FOR RELIABLE LOVE

All of us want reliable love.

We want somebody who will stick with us through thick and thin, somebody who will put up with our little foibles, somebody who will share our adventures, and somebody with whom we can grow old.

In short we need somebody to whom we can commit and who will commit to us.

But what does commitment mean?

And what does it look like?

Rhiannon's story

I'm thirty and happily married to Steve whom I met three years ago. We've just had our first child. But all of this only happened because I decided to leave Joe. I'd been with him for eight years. Our story shows the two sides of commitment. We were "committed" because from the outside we had a relationship that looked much like a married couple. But on the inside, we had much less idea where we were going. We were committed to one another whether we liked it or not. It took a lot to break free, even when it was increasingly obvious that the relationship was going nowhere.

We met online soon after I had left school. I thought I'd try out one of these dating agencies. It was pretty nerve-racking. But I'd just had some nice photos taken of me and I thought I'd try my luck.

Joe's photo stood out straight away. He was good looking, tanned and muscly, and a couple of years older than me.

Of course, I had no idea if we would connect and I was really nervous about meeting a complete stranger. So on our first date, I arranged for a friend to phone me at a strategic moment to check that I was all right. When we met up, I could see that he was physically shaking from his own nerves. I thought that was a good sign.

As well as finding him attractive physically, I liked that he was shy and therefore so different from me. I am outgoing, very much a party person. I like being active and around people.

Our relationship continued during my time at university. He would come and visit me from time to time and he came on holiday with my family. They liked him but quickly noticed that he seemed lacking in initiative. Whereas I and my parents are very proactive, always thinking ahead, he seemed not to spot when things needed doing, like cooking or washing-up. He seemed content in front of the telly.

So why did I stay with him? Because he was kind and because he was there. If I needed picking up at 3 a.m. from a party, he would happily come and pick me up without complaint.

After university, I found a really good job in the same town. Joe moved to be with me, found a job for himself, and bought a house. We moved in together.

For a while, I thought it was a good sign. After all he had shown initiative and that he cared for me in moving. But it soon became apparent that he was acting more out of self-interest. He referred very pointedly to the house or the car as his. He even made me pay rent.

I began to feel second-rate in our relationship. Things needed to change. I needed to see clearer signs that he valued me. Little things were beginning to bother me, whether it was persistently leaving his wet towel on the bed, or never calling me at work to find out how I was, or his habit of picking his nose. Whenever I told him I couldn't go further unless he sorted things out, he always sounded like he understood and agreed. He would plead with me and there were often tears. But nothing ever changed.

After three years of his dithering, I finally decided to leave. I should have done it sooner. But there seemed to be so many questions about where I would go and how he could stop me.

It just came to me one morning, in one of those light-bulb moments, that all I had to do was rent a car and a furnished apartment for a month. It would give me time to sort myself out.

So I actually did it, packing all my stuff and moving out while he was at work.

I wasn't going to just disappear without telling him. I'm not like that. So I waited for him to get back from work. He tried on his usual promise that he would change. I replied that he had never changed before so why should I believe him now? I'm gone, I said.

I don't think that was eight years wasted but I definitely should have left Joe a lot earlier. We had good times together and he was always kind, even if he was ultimately more interested in himself than in me. Apart from finding each other visually attractive, there simply wasn't enough to sustain us. We were too different.

Anyway, I spent the next few weeks fruitfully, reorganizing my life, working out what I would really need from a potential husband, and promising myself not to have any new relationship for a very long time.

I met Steve a month later.

I'm committed if you are

We hear a lot about commitment in the business world. Companies like to tell us how committed they are, for example, whether they are "delivering outstanding customer service", "providing the best prices" or "prioritizing safety".

But this doesn't sound quite like the kind of commitment we want in our relationships.

Companies may be signalling their good intentions to us. They might even follow up on their intentions and provide us with a good service or the best prices or keep us safe.

The problem is that we have to pay them to do it. If we stop paying them, their so-called commitment to us stops.

So what they mean by commitment is in fact *conditional*. All they're saying is that they will stick to their side of a contract so long as we stick to ours.

The kind of commitment we want is *unconditional*.

We want to be able to have our bad days and still know that somebody will stick around. This kind of commitment is much more of a promise, or a decision, or a plan of action. It depends much more on what *I* do, regardless of whether *you* do too.

Of course, there's not much point making an unconditional commitment to somebody if you don't think they will reciprocate. To that extent, unconditional commitment can seem incredibly risky and one-sided. That makes it easy to understand commitment-phobes, doesn't it?

But if we want reliable love from somebody else, they're going to have to take a chance on you every bit as much as you're going to take a chance on them.

No turning back

Every summer, we go on a family holiday to a small flat in Cornwall. Because we've been doing this for well over thirty years now, we have built up various traditions, things that we do every time we go. They're very familiar, very comfortable, and it would seem odd if we didn't do them.

One of those traditions is a long coastal walk. I look forward to it every year. But part of that walk is timing it so that the tide is right and we – or those of us who feel the need – can dive into a remote and rugged rock pool. If the tide is too low, there's not enough water. If too high, then the pool disappears.

Before my children dive in, I always check it's safe by diving in first. After all, this is a rock pool in the middle of nowhere. It seems deep enough and we've dived into it many times before. But rocks do get washed around. So there is a degree of risk. I also need to check our escape route and discuss how we are going to clamber out of the water across the seaweed and barnacle-encrusted rocks as the waves pour in and out. We always end up with minor cuts on our feet and legs. But that's part of the adventure. Finally, just outside the rock pool, up to half a dozen seal heads are bobbing up out of the sea, watching us. I really do not want to dive in and find I'm sharing a cold bath with a wild seal.

As I edge my toes over the sharp rocks and prepare to dive, I can't help but hesitate for a few seconds. Waves are pouring in. Wild seals are staring at us. I'm going to get cuts on my legs. But most of all, this is England. It's going to be cold!

As I lean forward, I pass through that critical moment when I realize I am committed. Now that there is no turning back, I put in maximum effort to make sure my dive is smooth and safe. Yes, there is a bit of a shock from the cold. But as I wave the others to come on in, I feel a huge sense of both achievement and relief. It's now the kids' turn to summon up their own courage and cross the commitment threshold for themselves.

This idea of "no turning back" is definitely a part of what it means to commit. It feels scary beforehand but once you've committed, you know you're in a better place.

But that isn't always the case with "no turning back".

When I get on a train, for example, I'm committing to a

journey. Once the doors lock, I can't get off. There's no turning back. And yet my train journeys feel quite different, depending on whether I'm setting off from home or heading back again.

When I'm heading away from home, I feel stuck. I'm on the train and committed to this journey whether I like it or not. But when I'm heading back towards home, I feel good. I have much to look forward to.

How can that be, when the commitment is the same, the experience of getting onboard the train is the same, the doors locking is the same, and the sense of "no turning back" is the same?

Somehow this is still not sufficient to explain what commitment means in relationships, because committing to another human being isn't a one-off event, although it's certainly part of it.

We might say we commit to one another when we get married. But this is just the beginning of our commitment. After all, we could change our mind the very next day, or the day after. It wouldn't be a very nice thing to do. It's as if we could decide not to dive even when in mid-air or decide to get off the train even as it pulls out of the station.

So there's an exit mechanism to commitment. Yet somehow most people who get married and make that commitment tend to keep their promise for life. They keep committing day after day, year after year, no matter what.

How does that work?

There's clearly more to commitment than meets the eye. And this is just me!

Happiness and commitment

People see commitment in an extraordinary array of different ways.

For example, one American study asked 250 adults across all age groups to come up with the different ways that they express their commitment. They produced over 900 different answers![1]

The very patient researchers then went through each of these answers and narrowed them down to ten different categories.

These ranged from expressing commitment to providing affection and support, showing respect, making an effort to communicate, working together on relationship problems, maintaining integrity, sharing companionship, and creating a positive atmosphere and a relational future.

They then asked another large group of people to say how often they used each of these categories in their own relationship, how long they saw their relationship lasting, how committed they were to it, and finally how happy they were.

Unsurprisingly, those who had made a formal commitment – that is, those who were engaged or married – reported using more of these behaviours compared with those who were only casually dating. Also, those who were engaged saw their commitment especially in terms of affection and talk about a future. Once married, however, couples appear not to use these particular methods so much to indicate their commitment.

Maybe more surprisingly, how long couples had been together – whether months or years – had no bearing on how often couples reported these behaviours overall. In other words, people don't stop showing their commitment to one another. They keep on doing it, just in different ways, as I suggested earlier.

In addition, women reported doing slightly more of everything than men. Well, what can I say? Are women more expressive about their commitment or are men just more modest about what they do?

OK, wrong answer... I will take cover! We'll come back to gender differences in the next chapter.

What is especially illuminating about this study is how relationship happiness and relationship commitment seem to be related to quite different behaviours. So the signs of happiness are not necessarily the same as the signs of commitment.

Hold that thought because it's important and I'm going to elaborate on it very shortly.

Relationship happiness seemed to be most closely linked to "companionship". This is pretty much what my wife Kate and I found when we conducted a survey of 300 mums for our last book *What Mums Want and Dads Need To Know*.[2] We found that being friends, being interested, and being kind were the top three things that mums wanted from dads. Put another way, that sounds like companionship to me.

Relationship commitment – how long people saw their relationship lasting and wanted it to last – seemed to depend more on whether couples expressed their commitment, talked about the future, and thought integrity was important. To me, these are issues of trust, openness and honesty that seem to reflect character more than anything else.

We'll talk about these in chapter 5 when we talk about the idea of "marriageability".

Dedication and constraints

If you're confused by all of this, don't worry.

I'm going to introduce you to the work of three of my favourite researchers anywhere in the world, Professors Scott Stanley, Howard Markman, and Galena Rhoades at the University of Denver.

In my view, they have done more than anyone to unlock the secrets of commitment and explain how it all works. Their work revolves around two simple ideas.

The first is *dedication and constraints*, which we'll deal with in this chapter.[3] The second is *sliding, deciding, and inertia*, which we'll deal with in the next chapter.[4]

To understand their version of what commitment means, let's consider a fairly typical relationship.

It begins with two people meeting each other. They like the look of each other and enjoy each other's company. As they spend more time together, their relationship grows.

At some point, they let their friends and family know that they are a couple. Most couples today sleep with one another fairly early on in the relationship. Most also move in to live together, get married, and have children together, though not necessarily in that order.

Over time they build a life together, a family identity, a social network of friends, and a shared relational and financial history together.

Dedication is the internal bond that holds them together as a couple. It reflects the extent to which two people *want to be* together, they see themselves as a couple, and they see a future for themselves together.

Constraints are the external bonds that make it harder for them to leave. They reflect the extent to which two people *have to be* together, as their life becomes ever more complex and entangled.

In their words:

> *Dedication refers to the desire of an individual to maintain or improve the quality of his or her relationship for the joint benefit of the participants. It is evidenced by a desire (and associated behaviors) not only to continue in the relationship, but also to improve it, to sacrifice for it, to invest in it, to link personal goals to it, and to seek the partner's welfare, not simply one's own.*
>
> *In contrast, constraint commitment refers to forces that constrain individuals to maintain relationships regardless of their personal dedication to them. Constraints may arise from either external or internal pressures, and they favor relationship stability by making termination of a relationship more economically, socially, personally, or psychologically costly.[5]*

My walled garden

Here's a picture that I have in my mind to show how commitment works.

Think about two people who want to grow a garden together in an imaginary and boundless field.

At first they begin with just a few seeds or flowers. After planting, they step back and admire their handiwork. It feels good.

To show anyone coming by that this is their patch, they mark out the territory around their new little flowerbed. Maybe they put a rope around the outside or just bang some posts in the ground at the corners.

One or two friends and family stop by and show their appreciation of the flowerbed. They recognize that a new garden could be in the making.

Before long, the couple realize they are spending more and more time in their garden, putting in new plants and nurturing them together. They really like this new garden. It's pretty obvious that they need to do a bit more than merely mark out their territory. They need to protect it by putting up a proper fence.

Because the couple enjoy being in the garden together so much, the fence makes them feel safe inside.

More of their friends and family gather around the outside of the fence and admire the fledgling garden within. The fence makes the onlookers realize that these two are probably not going to be interested in gardening with anyone else.

On the inside, the couple like seeing their friends and family gazing in. It doesn't occur to them that they might ever want to stop gardening together. But if it ever did come to the point that it wasn't so much fun any more, the fence they have now put in around them would make it just a little bit harder to stop and leave.

That wasn't why they did it, of course. They did it to protect their garden space. But the very fact that it's there now encourages them to stick at it.

And on their garden grows. As they plant more and more, and they begin to realize that they want this garden to last, they decide to replace the fence with a much stronger, sturdier, wall.

Now the garden has become a walled garden.

It's pretty clear that this is the only place they are going to do their gardening, they can think far into the future, which means they can plant trees together and really plan out the design of the garden and the way they do things.

The relationship as a garden

You can see where I've taken you with this.

The garden represents *dedication* – the "wanting to stay together" part of commitment.

The fence or wall around the garden represents *constraints* – the "having to stay together" part of commitment.

A relationship – just like a garden – begins with small steps, establishing that two people like spending time together and working out when they will next meet.

At some point, the couple establishes a boundary around their relationship – like a fence – and tell their friends and family what's going on.

These are the first signs of both *dedication* and *constraints*, both of which grow over time.

In terms of *dedication*, two individuals are establishing a new identity for themselves as a couple: *we* rather than just "*you* and *me*". They also develop a sense of future, initially just looking a few days ahead until the next date, but then looking weeks ahead to think about weekends or family visits, and months ahead for holidays or Christmas.

The garden is a fun place to be.

In terms of *constraints*, every time they pass through a stage in their relationship – beginning dating, announcing themselves to the world as an established couple, moving in together, having children – they give themselves more affirmation in their new identity as a couple, and ultimately as a family. Having friends and family around who think of them as a couple feels good. Moving in together feels like a new deeper stage of their relationship, and that feels good. Having children definitely affirms them as the co-founders of a new family. And that's good too.

The fence around them makes them feel safe.

And of course, there's marriage. Although marriage adds the *constraints* of enhanced social and legal status, which ties them in to the relationship just that little bit more, marriage is mostly about *dedication*. It's the ultimate step. In getting married they are deciding to spend the rest of their lives together; they're telling the world that this is their plan, and they're identifying themselves with a new social and legal status.

They're saying, "We love our garden so much that we have walled ourselves in."

Timing matters: Dedication before constraints

This *dedication and constraints* model of commitment is incredibly helpful for understanding how relationships work.

Dedication is obviously important: being a couple and having a sense of future. But so are *constraints*: being affirmed by your friends, having a shared history, living together, having children.

But how do they influence our chances of finding reliable love? Is one of these more important than the other? Or are they both equally important?

For some years now, our friends in the US have been regularly surveying a group of around 1,200 men and women, all of whom were initially aged between eighteen and thirty-five, unmarried and in a romantic relationship. Some already had children while others didn't, and some have had them since. Some of these young adults have subsequently married while others haven't, and of course some have split up.

In one of the first studies to look at this group early on, Professor Galena Rhoades and her colleagues wanted to see how the different aspects of commitment influenced the chances of these young couples staying together over an eight-month period.[6]

The simple answer is that both *dedication* and *constraints* had a unique impact.

How strongly couples wanted to be together told them a lot about whether they were still together eight months later. That was the influence of *dedication*.

How much couples had invested together, how much social pressure they felt to stay together, and how much they felt trapped or not, also revealed a lot of information. That was the influence of *constraints*.

This study is interesting because it shows how "wanting to be together" and "having to be together" each independently affect the chances of young couples actually staying together, albeit over a relatively short space of time.

In other words, building the garden wall has just as much impact on stability as how much you want to grow the garden.

That should flash warning signs for those who believe that moving in together early on in a relationship is risk-free.

Here's another commitment analogy for you. Moving in together is a bit like getting in a car and going for a drive. The question is whether "wanting to be together" in the car is greater or lesser than "having to be together" for the journey.

Being in a car and driving along feels good when you both want to be there in the first place. The *constraint* of being in a car that has already travelled some distance feels good because the *dedication* or desire to be on a journey together is also strong.

But when you've got into the car before figuring out whether you really want to be there for the long haul, the experience can quickly feel like a trap. After even a short journey away from home, you suddenly realize that it's harder than you thought to abandon the car.

Or let's go back to the garden analogy. When things are going well, we're thinking about the garden and the fence feels protective and affirming. It makes us feel safe and secure in the way we've chosen to live our lives.

But when the garden becomes less appealing, we become more aware of the fence or wall looming large around us, blocking us in, constraining our options, stopping us from making a different life, and making us feel trapped.[7]

Not surprisingly, several studies have now shown that couples who move in together before getting engaged tend to have less happy subsequent marriages than those who move in after engagement or marriage. This isn't always the case but it is for a significant minority, maybe one in four couples. We'll discuss this more in the next chapter.[8]

Although most of these studies were conducted in the US where a significant proportion of couples still delay moving in until they are engaged, I am well aware that almost all couples in the UK now move in early on as a matter of routine.

Nonetheless the point should be clear: moving in together early in a relationship is not risk-free. Timing matters.[9]

If you want reliable love, it's best to figure out where you're going before you get in the car!

CHAPTER 3

DECIDE OR SLIDE?*

Making a decision is the foundation stone of any activity where you have a particular goal in mind.

You decide, you make a plan, and you're intentional and deliberate in how you carry it out.

Some good things in life happen by accident. But most things happen because somebody made the effort to make them happen. They made a decision and a plan. They made it happen.

Why should relationships be any different?

Decisions affect the way we behave

When I make a decision to do something, usually – though by no means always – it means I'll complete the job or task. I've made my mind up. I've made a plan. I've bought into the idea of doing something. So now I'm going to give it my best shot. I'll probably enjoy doing it. I'll take major obstacles seriously and won't worry too much about minor obstacles. One way or another, I'll get the job done.

As a very simple example, I had to clean the moss off part of a corrugated roof at our home recently. Moss had been building up for a few years and was clogging the gutter whenever it rained. I'd known for a long time that the job needed doing, but I'd kept putting it off.

One day last winter, I just decided to do it. So I got a ladder,

---

*   With credit to Scott Stanley and his team at the University of
     Denver for coining this handy phrase.

a couple of planks of wood to stop me falling through the roof, some gloves, a rake, and a broom.

The job wasn't especially easy. It was dirty, hard work. And it was also physically uncomfortable shuffling along the planks on my knees across an angled roof, while making sure I didn't slither off and disappear over the edge.

From both above and below, I angled the end of the rake to push or pull the moss out of each line of corrugated gutter. I then used my hands to clear the mess before brushing the roof down with the broom. There were moments when I wondered if I should get a builder or roofer to do the job professionally. But no, I thought. I can do this.

After a couple of hours, the job was done. The roof now looks great and the main gutter drains properly without getting clogged. I felt suitably pleased with myself and I even quite enjoyed doing it. I certainly enjoyed the results.

I'd decided and I did it.

However, if I go into something half-heartedly, I'll usually go along with it. If I haven't fully engaged with it, I don't feel quite as committed. It doesn't seem to matter so much if I don't complete the job or if I walk away. I'm then less likely to enjoy it and more likely to give up half-way through.

As an example of this, I'm really not a big fan of family games. For whatever reason, they just don't do it for me. But my family loves games. So at Christmas time, I go along with the charades or whatever it is that we are playing. I'm not exactly gritting my teeth and hating it. But I join in because I have to. My father-in-law had a perfect expression for this: enforced fun!

One of the games we play is the one where you have a series of cards with names of people or things or actions or events. You have to describe the word on each card to your team without saying the word itself. The aim is to help your team name as many words as possible correctly within a minute. The game brings out the competitive streak in all of us, including me. However, since most of my family seem to be much better at this than I am, I really don't enjoy the game as much as they seem to.

Anyway, as I gradually lose interest in the game, I can easily find an excuse to drift away and do something else, like a bit of washing-up, or topping up drinks, or even checking mindlessly through my phone.

In these situations, because I've not really engaged with the game, I tend not to enjoy it as much as I might. I also know that it's easy to walk away if I feel like it or if things aren't going well.

Instead of deciding, I'm sliding.

Sliding doesn't guarantee failure. In fact, there are plenty of times when I start out by sliding into doing something and deciding to engage fully when the activity is underway.

For example, each summer my wife Kate hosts an event for a local charity. But since this means opening up our house and garden to lots of guests, it also means making the place look lovely. Kate's idea of lovely is far more creative and visionary and impressive than mine. So the preparation seems to involve a lot more effort and – to me – more unnecessary little touches than I would have done.

But I have to admit when the day finally arrives and the tent is up and tea served, it is always a terrific day. From merely going along with her plan, I now actively engage with it. The result is that I always enjoy the day much more than I expected to. And Kate is relieved that I have made an effort to help out and make the day a success.

To succeed at anything, at some point you have to make a decision.

Deciding, being intentional, and setting goals

My wife Kate has an amazing friend whom I'll call Tara. But Kate is only friends with Tara because Tara was so intentional about becoming friends. They met a few years ago when we were on holiday with our children and another family. Our family had been out for the morning and got back in time for a late lunch. That was when we met Tara, who was an old friend of the other family.

Alas, Tara had to leave thirty minutes later. Yet within that thirty minutes, Kate and Tara clicked. They connected and took contact details.

In most circumstances, it's all too easy to imagine how this could have ended up as nothing more than a nice encounter. After all there are lots of people in the world who could be friends with us. But time and opportunities are always limited. So friendships are often limited to those who live near you or long-time friends that you bump into every decade or so and continue chatting as if you'd seen them yesterday.

Given that Tara lives in Spain, it seemed that this nice encounter was unlikely to blossom into anything more. We would love to have been friends but, realistically, it was never going to happen.

But Tara, as we now know, is very intentional about what she wants. That thirty minutes was sufficient for her to decide she wanted to be friends with us, well, with Kate in particular. She initiated an exchange of emails, then a video chat, and then a plan to come to see us and for us to see them.

And that's exactly what has happened. A wonderful friendship has developed out of a brief introduction because Tara made a decision to make it happen.

Some good things only happen with a plan.

Things like businesses, holidays, going on a diet, getting fit, or having family gatherings don't happen by accident. They happen because somebody makes a decision, sets some goals, takes responsibility, and then follows it up with a plan.

As our children have progressed through their teenage years, we've faced the same problem that most parents face: a child coming up to exams who seems to be coasting.

Just a few years ago, one of my boys was spending a great deal of his time on a computer game. Kate and I talked to him about it several times, suggesting he set time limits so he got his work done and curfews so he got enough sleep. We would help and encourage him with this but wouldn't monitor him. After all he had to make his own decisions.

It was obvious that he knew there was a problem but he was defensive whenever we brought the subject up.

With six months to go, we had one more go at trying to persuade him to cut back on the gaming. We reminded him that it was only a few months before the exams. He was a bright boy who should be able to do well. But he would be only disappointed in himself if he fell short. He would know that. We affirmed how proud he would be if he prepared properly and did his best. Whatever the results, he would know he had given it a good try.

One evening, he came down. He was clearly quite emotional as he told us he had uninstalled the game and wanted help with a revision plan. He did well in his exams because he had made a decision. Of course, we're proud of our children whatever they do, even when they blow it. But it's especially heart-warming when they do something really smart like our son did.

Sliding and deciding in relationships

So what makes us think marriage and relationships are any different?

Making decisions, or not, has a similarly profound effect on the way we think about our relationships and behave towards others.

In the last chapter, we looked at the structure of how couples commit, through *dedication* to one another on the inside but also through *constraints* on the outside.

There's also a process to commitment. And it involves deciding, sliding, and inertia.[1]

Every time we move to the next stage of a relationship – whether getting together in the first place, telling friends and family, living together, getting married, having children – we can either decide or slide.

When we decide, we make a plan. We make things clear and explicit.

When we slide, we go with the flow. This may be part of an eventual plan or it may not. We leave things open-ended.

When we get together, we may have an idea in our minds about where we want the relationship to go. So we discuss some of the things we need or want, such as whether this is just fun with possibilities or has a destination from the start. That's deciding. But maybe we don't have a clear idea, which makes it hard to discuss. We just want to see how things turn out. That's sliding.

When we tell friends and family, it might be because they found out by accident. We were caught together and admitted it. We didn't have a plan. That's sliding. But maybe we decided we were going to ring our parents and tell them, or text some key friends. In which case we decided.

When we live together, it might be a deliberate step. We decided whether and how we should make the transition before it happened naturally. But it might just have kind of happened. There was no particular plan. We just slid into living together.

Even though getting married would seem to require a clear decision, as we shall see with Peter and Elena's story later in this chapter, it is quite possible to end up married because of social or family pressure – to slide into marriage.

Whether we decide or slide, every time we pass through a relationship transition, we increase the level of inertia in the relationship. Inertia in physics makes things harder to move. Inertia in relationships makes it harder to leave, should you wish to do so.

So here's the crux of my whole book.

As relationships grow, constraints inevitably increase. More constraints mean more inertia. More inertia means fewer choices.

When I am surrounded by friends, family, children, home, belongings, memories, plans, and lack of alternatives, my choice of whether to stay in the relationship or not is limited.

That's a good thing if both of us have clearly decided it was what we both wanted. It may not be quite so good if I'd found myself here having never quite planned or even expected it.

It was thrust upon me. I slid into it. And now I'm stuck.

So let's have a look at some real-life couples and how they handle the growing inertia in their relationships.

In both cases, it's the man who struggles to decide. This reflects real life pretty well. Of course, there are also women who can't decide – Anna's story in chapter 1 is a real-life example – it's just a lot less common.

Sarah's story

I met David soon after leaving university. Although I realized very early on that he was the man I wanted to marry, he took rather longer to come around to the idea. Our relationship drifted aimlessly for three years with him unwilling to commit to me. It was only after I made the decision to break up with him that he was able to make the decision to propose. I think this is interesting because it really shows how people can change their minds for the better. It was only when David could make a decision for himself that we were able to replace years of anxiety and turmoil with peace and confidence in our future together.

The funny thing is that he was the one driving the relationship right at the beginning.

After our first meeting, we got on really well and began dating in the old-fashioned sense. But we only had a few weeks before both of us moved to different towns to embark on new careers after university. Although I really enjoyed his company, I wasn't physically attracted to him. I didn't see where the relationship was going so I assumed it would just fizzle out. I wasn't prepared to give up my career plan for him. It would have been too much of a risk so early on.

Yet he was the one that wanted to make the relationship work. And it was he that kept in touch with me over the following year. Eventually his work brought him to the same town as me. I was pretty excited about this and agreed to meet up. We got on well and saw each other a couple of times a week for the next few months.

I'm quite a strong-minded and decisive person so I was quite quick to see the long-term potential in this relationship. But when I started to talk about marriage, I could sense he was uncomfortable. Whereas I couldn't see the point of a relationship if it wasn't heading in that direction, he was a lot more wary and uncertain.

We were clearly very different. I could see that if we married, I would be willing to drop whatever necessary to make our relationship work. He still wanted the flexibility to be able to do what he wanted without being limited by a relationship.

Our relationship bumbled on for two years, with me feeling increasingly miserable that he wouldn't commit and him feeling miserable that I was. I so wanted him to be content with his life, and of course to marry me! It didn't help that my career began to take off whereas his was struggling to get off the ground.

I knew he loved me. But he just thought differently to me. I thought we should just get on with it and work at life as a married couple. He wanted to be more sure. I didn't really care if he married me under duress or not. So I kept pushing him to make a decision even though I could see it made him extremely uncomfortable.

There was no way I was going to break up with him. The ball was entirely in his court to commit or quit. He quit. It wasn't the decision I wanted. But it was good that he did it. He told me how much he loved me but he couldn't do this any more. I knew both these things were true. So we split.

It was a painful time. I don't think I was completely heartbroken because I could rationalize why he left. It made sense.

Of course, I couldn't stop thinking about him. What I didn't know was that he also couldn't stop thinking about me. I'm so grateful to his friends and family for the way they listened to him and didn't impose solutions on him. He'd had plenty of that from me.

At some point during our six months apart, he must have realized that the only way back was if he asked me to marry him. Just going back to our old relationship was a non-starter.

Freed from the pressure to talk about our relationship, we had a couple of lovely, happy phone conversations. He told me how much he missed me. I felt the same.

So we decided to meet up again, during which time he didn't quite propose but made it clear that he would. Although friends and family on both sides expressed concern about us getting back together without a plan, we knew that we had one. He was just waiting for the right time, which came a few weeks later.

In the run up to the wedding, we had some very difficult conversations where he told me how clear he was about the decision but also how his feelings of turmoil had all come flooding back. I didn't freak out because I knew I had to trust him, even to the point that I thought I could cope if he changed his mind walking up the aisle.

Having won my man, I should have been thrilled. Instead it was my turn to crumple with doubts on the first night of our honeymoon. But David was so gentle and reassuring, joking that now I'd got him, I could hardly run off home.

The following morning, our marriage began. It was like a leaf-blower had blown away all the rain and debris, the sun had come out, and our path was now clear.

We've been married for three years now and I've never been happier. I think that if we hadn't split up, our marriage would never have worked. But he made the decision to leave and he made the decision to marry me. I had to lose him to win him.

Peter's story

> *Elena and I are married and have two young children. Stupidly I had an affair. Elena has only recently found out and is obviously distraught. I think she was doubly shocked when I told her I'd felt steamrollered into marriage in the first place. Elena is an amazing woman and wants to forgive me and get our marriage back. But I find it hard making decisions about the future, which is exactly what I have to do if we want to make our marriage work properly for the first time.*

I first met Elena through a church group. My job was in the growing field of computers and IT. Elena was the administrator at a primary school. Both of us fell in love pretty quickly. We spent every opportunity that we could outside work together.

Elena started slipping the subject of marriage into our conversations within a few months. I think I fitted the bill for her. I'm a pretty straight sort of guy, I work hard, and I'm a people pleaser. I try to be kind to those around me. I always wanted Elena to feel special.

As we headed toward the end of our first year together, marriage came up almost every time we talked. I enjoyed the way we were as a couple but didn't want to be rushed into anything. I wanted to take my time, to make sure.

Although the subject made me feel squirmy and uncomfortable, I could usually palm it off with laughter, as if I felt the same way as she did. It wasn't that I didn't love her. I did. I just wasn't so convinced that our entire lives and future should be so clearly defined.

Eventually Elena's persistence paid off and, rather sheepishly, I proposed. I think she thought my reticence was sweet, or humble, or shy or something. It wasn't. In trying not to hurt her, I was pretending I wanted something I wasn't yet ready for. In a way, it was a lie.

Of course, as soon as we made the news public, the marriage train gathered an unstoppable momentum. There was now no way for me to get off.

Although Elena was clearly thrilled to have reached her goal, I spent the first six months of our marriage in turmoil. I loved Elena but I'd also deceived her.

I wasn't as wedded to our marriage as she was, and thought I was.

Now that I was resigned to my situation – I certainly wasn't unhappy enough to want a divorce – I was definitely on the way to buying in, to making a decision that this was my choice too. I could have gone from being a slider to decider.

Our two children were born before we had completed three years of marriage. Elena adored being a mum and her passion for family life consumed her. It was all we talked about.

As her focus narrowed to the children and the exclusion of all else, my love for her changed into a sense of duty. I suppose I neglected her as much as she seemed to neglect me.

The affair with a work colleague began innocently enough with a glance and a smile, before moving on to chats over the office coffee machine, flirty looks, and then a hand on my arm. I could have stopped it, but I didn't. There were so many little red lines that were crossed. Going for a drink after work was one of the worst. But having crossed the line once, it was easier to cross again and again. Over drinks, I relaxed and told her the full story. At last I felt understood. One thing led to another.

Our children were at primary school and Elena and I had been married for ten years when she found out. She was devastated because the possibility simply hadn't occurred to her. Family was so important to her that it had to be for me too.

We went to see some older married friends who were very non-judgmental. Elena cried a lot. I felt numb but held her hand throughout. I almost wanted her to scream at me and tell me she never wanted to see me again. I deserved it because I'd betrayed her. But instead she just kept telling me she loved me and wanted to sort it out. She looked so hurt and confused.

I'm still living with Elena, though we sleep in different rooms. The one decision I've made so far is to end the affair. I could somehow justify it to myself so long as it was kept in the dark. I wasn't overtly hurting Elena.

Elena would be more than justified in kicking me out. But she hasn't. Her commitment to me is astonishing. I know she really needs me to make a decision once and for all, whether to leave so that she can have a fresh start or to stay and buy into the marriage once and for all, to commit to it as strongly as she does.

The ball is in my court. I need to decide, not slide, though I'm not sure I'm ready yet. I hope I can summon up the courage to do it one day.

Men and decisions

In this chapter we've seen some of the anecdotal evidence that making decisions makes success more likely. If I make a clear decision, I'm more likely to do and enjoy doing things that I needed to do but didn't especially want to do – like clearing moss from a roof or co-hosting an event with my wife! We've seen examples of a decision to develop a friendship or pass an exam. And we've seen examples from relationships of people who struggled with decisions and paid the price and those who made a decision with much more positive consequences.

But I've also hinted that, for success in relationships, decisions are especially important to men. What's the evidence for this?

After all, one of the big recent themes in politics, the media, and research is inequality between men and women. As a man with a wife and four daughters, I have no truck with those who think women can't achieve as much as men.

Although there are clear differences between men and women, I argued strongly in my last book *What Mums Want and Dads Need to Know*[2] – co-authored with my wife Kate – that male and female differences are mostly a question of overlap rather than absolute differences. While it may be the case that men tend to do better in maths and sciences, and hence dominate sectors such as engineering, and women tend to do better in social subjects, and hence dominate sectors such as care, these are issues of overlap.

However, there is one area where men and women indisputably differ. And that is in the matter of who gives birth. Because only women experience the biology and psychology of pregnancy and childbirth, it shouldn't be surprising to find significant differences between how men and women are hard-wired into the way they operate their relationships at home.

One of these differences is that women's commitment seems to be more connected with attachment while men's commitment seems to be more about decision-making.

So let's have a look at the hard evidence, much of which comes from studies of commitment in marriage and cohabitation conducted by the Denver researchers.

It was only as recently as 2004 that the results of the first specific study of *dedication* – how important your relationship is, how much of a future you see in it, how much you think about "us" rather than "you" or "me", and how strong you plan to be in the rough times – was published.

Scott Stanley and colleagues compared data on hundreds of married and cohabiting couples who had been together for five years or less. What they found was that the married men were significantly more dedicated and satisfied with their relationship than the unmarried men. This was not the case for the women, where there were no differences.[3]

This evidence demonstrates that men seem to be happier and more committed if they are married. Of course, that doesn't tell us whether it was marriage that made the difference or merely that those who were already committed then got married. But what it does tell us is that women's commitment is more about the moving in and not the marriage.

On average at least, men and women see commitment differently.

At the same time, Galena Rhoades had conducted a smaller study that suggests the dividing line for dedication was not when couples got married, but when couples got engaged. She found that those who had lived together before getting engaged were subsequently also less committed once they were married.[4]

Think about this for a second.

Getting married is not the moment that you make your commitment. Hopefully you've already made your mind up by that point. No, the wedding is the time when you formally recognize the commitment you've already made, and celebrate it in front of others.

Getting engaged is when you make the real commitment, when you decide.

On average at least, couples who move in together before they have made the decision to marry are subsequently less committed than those who decide to marry before moving in.

A couple of years later Galena published the key study that tied these two points together.

Among 200 couples who had been married for an average of four years, some had moved in before getting engaged and some afterwards. But the average level of commitment was very similar for all of these groups except for the men who had moved in before getting engaged.[5]

Here was the first really clear evidence that men's commitment is tied to the decision to commit, rather than the act of moving in, as it seems to be for women.[6]

Going back to whether it's the committed men that tend to get married or marriage that makes men more committed, neither of these answers is quite right.

What is happening is that it's the men who make a decision that are more committed. Marriage usually represents a decision. But of course, as we've seen with the stories from David and Peter above, it all boils down to whether they decide or slide.

Deciding to live together?

Although marriage is the ultimate step of dedication, there are other signs that point the way.

One of my favourite studies from the Denver team is when they followed the group of 1,200 young unmarried adults over an eight-month period. I mentioned this study in the last chapter because it showed how both *dedication* and *constraints* influence stability.[7]

But what's more practical about the study is that it highlights how specific acts of commitment improve the chances of staying together, at least in the short term.

These include paying for each other's debt, getting a pet together, sharing a gym membership, and buying a house together.

All of these are constraints that make it harder to leave a relationship, should either party want to do so. But they also reflect a decision to do something together that involves some sense of future. Using our garden analogy, they may raise the size of the fence. But they also reflect a desire to build the garden.

Notably absent from the list of predictors are whether couples live together and whether they have a child together. If you see these in the lives of friends that you know, you can't use them to draw a conclusion that they are committed.

Why?

Because having a baby and moving in together can both "just kind of happen". They don't necessarily require a decision. As many parents will attest, you can slide into having a baby. And you can certainly slide into living together.

One American study found that nearly half of all couples who lived together did not make a deliberate decision to do so. One third of couples couldn't even agree on a start date within three months of one another.[8]

And our own UK research at Marriage Foundation shows that just half of births to cohabiting couples are planned compared with three quarters of births to married couples. So it's just as easy to slide into parenthood as it is to decide.[9]

It took me a while to sort out. But I eventually managed to encourage *The Telegraph* newspaper to run a story with this wonderful tagline: "Getting a pet is a better sign that a young unmarried couple will stay together than having a baby, it has been claimed."[10] Ha!

Men and goals

There's one more line of evidence that supports this idea that men respond especially well to decisions, and it's in the study of goal-setting.

Researchers at a Dutch university persuaded a large group of first-year students to attend a couple of goal-setting classes. The students were encouraged to think about personal habits they'd like to improve and where they saw themselves a few years on, as well as the future they'd like to avoid if bad habits took them down a wrong path. They then set some specific goals and wrote them down beneath a professional portrait photo.[11]

The net result was that the male students made significant gains in their overall study results by the end of the second year, which were sustained through the third year.

Female students, who to be fair tend to do better anyway, did not make significant gains.

This intervention looks remarkably similar to getting people to think about deciding or sliding. And the results look similar as well.

Just as young men tend to be less committed at marriage unless they make a clear goal-oriented decision, young men tend to perform less well at university unless they make a clear goal-oriented decision.

Deciding matters for men.

CHAPTER 4

DO YOU LOVE ME?

> When we begin a relationship, we dance carefully around one another, putting our best foot forward, trying to impress, wary of blowing it with a wrong comment or move.
>
> Yet throughout this long dance, a nagging doubt lingers in the back of our minds.
>
> "Does she love me?"
>
> "Does he love me?"
>
> "Do you love me?"
>
> An essential ingredient of any successful relationship is the resolution of this underlying anxiety and ambiguity. It could take months. It could take years. But at some stage, what we all need is clarity.

How it all began for us

I first met Kate when I was a young Royal Navy commando pilot on a junior staff course at the Royal Naval College at Greenwich, London. The course was deeply dull, to me anyway. But having spent much of the previous two years on what seemed like a perpetual cycle of winters spent outdoors – Dartmoor, the Falkland Islands, two trips to Norway – the prospect of a few weeks indoors in London seemed like a good deal.

Parties in the crypt of the famous Painted Hall, now part of the University of Greenwich, were a regular highlight.

It was at a Valentine's Day party that I met Kate. A fellow naval officer, to whom I am forever grateful, had invited her along, presumably with the aim of furthering his own relationship with her. Luckily for me, that relationship hadn't properly begun before she and I were introduced. We hit it off immediately and chatted and danced the night away. To be honest, my memory of the party is somewhat hazy. However, in a moment of clarity, I did remember to complete the most important task of the evening, which was to obtain Kate's phone number.

What I also remember with vivid clarity was the apprehension I then felt at making the first follow-up phone call. Kate was lovely and I really wanted to meet up with her again. Through our first few conversations and evenings out together, excitement at the prospect of winning her as my girlfriend alternated all too uncomfortably with the fear of missing out and losing her to someone else.

I can only liken my subdued anxiety to the same sort of feeling I felt when we were buying the home we now live in. Until there's some sort of clarity, we're living in a world of uncertainty and ambiguity, where things could go either way. I didn't want to get my hopes up too high in case things fell through. But, on the other hand, it was hard to contain those hopes. They were sky high.

At some point, we kissed. It established us as boyfriend and girlfriend and was the first rung of the relationship ladder. It meant fun and laughter and joy, as well as a sense of relief at having not lost out. But although it swept away the first layer of uncertainty, it wasn't long before I realized there were more layers to come. After all, the first rung of the ladder is just that: the first rung.

Actually, in our case, I always felt supremely confident that we would get married. I don't know why I did – I just did. This was the early to mid-1980s and although living together was becoming more common, in our family it was not an alternative to marriage. If you loved someone, you married them.

Kate felt similarly about marriage, but was not nearly as certain as I was that marriage was our inevitable conclusion. On one occasion after we had been together for about eighteen months, I stopped her suddenly while we were out on a walk.

"I've got a very important question to ask you," I told her. Kate's heart skipped a beat, convinced that I was about to propose. "Did you bring the car keys with you?"

I had no idea I had unintentionally caused such a surge of excited anticipation and then disappointment in Kate. I thought I was just being funny. Kate only told me about this after we finally got engaged a few months later.

What it highlighted was that Kate and I had achieved some clarity about our future relationship but not about its timing. Both of us were beginning to see ourselves as a married couple. We had talked about it in the way that couples do, referring to the "M-word".

Ambiguity and asymmetry

Although there was a degree of unspoken ambiguity about how we would get there, Kate and I found ways to communicate to each other that we were equally committed; that one day we would get married. And one day we did.

For many couples, however, one person may be more committed – that is, dedicated – than the other. The more committed one thinks about them as a team, a couple with a future. The less committed one is enjoying the now and isn't yet thinking about their future.

This may just be a question of timing. One person concludes that this is it. The other takes a little longer to get there.

We've already seen some clues that it is typically men who take a little longer to commit. As a broad generalization, women tend to commit when they move in, whereas men tend to commit only when they have made their mind up for certain.

So it could simply be that one person is a little further ahead. Given time, the other will catch up.

Or it may indicate a more serious problem, a mismatch of expectations. This is what's called asymmetric commitment.

Alas there aren't many studies that have looked at this subject.

In the UK, a survey by the counselling organization Relate found that 15% of those in unmarried relationships – cohabiting or not – worried that their partner was not as committed as they were. Not surprisingly, only 6% of those in married relationships were also worried.[1]

This question is important, in that it measures a perceived imbalance of commitment. If I don't think you are as committed as I am, then this is clearly a genuine concern.

But it's quite possible that some people might worry about their partner's commitment when there's no need. In which case, this is not a question of asymmetry but of ambiguity.

Do you see the difference? There may not be a problem of commitment. It's more a problem of confidence. This could be down to poor communication: they just haven't talked about it. Or it could be a lack of clarity: they haven't signalled their intent clearly enough.

In our first year of going out together, Kate and I might easily have said we were worried about the other's commitment. Up until the moment that we got engaged, there was obviously some degree of uncertainty about our future path. Although we talked about the "M-word", it wasn't guaranteed. We were still checking each other out.

As we danced our dance around one another, there was one genuinely nerve-racking moment when it looked like we might split up. Kate was definitely worried about my apparent indifference to her at times. But when she challenged me on this and saw my fear that she would leave me, she then saw how committed I was to her. Obviously, I needed to show that more. But it re-established us as a couple and it wasn't long after that that we got engaged.

So either of us would have been right to worry about the other's commitment. But this was a question of ambiguity and not asymmetry.

Still with me?

As well as the difference between married and cohabiting people, there is one more interesting finding in the Relate study. Slightly more women expressed worry about their partner's commitment than men. We found that 10% of women expressed this worry compared with 8% of men.

This 2% gap may not seem very big. But when you think that the vast majority of adult couples in any sample will be married, where there was less worry about commitment, then a small overall gap between women and men almost certainly reflects a much bigger gender gap in the remaining minority unmarried group.[2]

This would definitely chime with what we discussed in the previous chapter. In relationships that haven't yet become formalized, men are more likely than women to be the ones who are less committed.

The existence of relationships where commitment is asymmetric has been documented in a number of American studies. At least half a dozen of these have also shown that asymmetric commitment is linked to lower quality relationships and a higher risk of splitting up.[3]

We'll come back to this shortly.

But, as ever, the only studies that look at the gender gap in commitment are from Galena Rhoades, Scott Stanley and colleagues in Denver.

The most recent of these is especially relevant to this book because it concerns young unmarried couples who had typically been together for a little over two years.[4]

Altogether 35% of these 315 couples could be described as asymmetric, where one partner had a relatively high level of commitment and the other a relatively low level. In 23% of couples, it was the man who was the less committed and in 12% it was the woman.

What happens to asymmetric couples?

The first thing, as mentioned above, is that asymmetric couples are less likely to have a happy relationship and more likely to split up than those who are more equally committed to one another.

The above sample of 315 couples is part of the larger study that has followed unmarried adults over five years. So that's how they knew who stayed together and who split up within that period.

And this asymmetry doesn't have to be real. As in the UK Relate study, US studies have shown that the perception that there is a problem means that there *will* be one.[5]

The second thing is that having somebody in the relationship who is less committed – whether one or both partners – puts the relationship at risk.

That is especially true for women. So women who are not especially committed seem more willing to pull the plug on the relationship.

However, if it is the man who is less committed, the relationship is likely to keep going.

This finding fits well with the idea that less committed men are "sliders" rather than "deciders". Not only is it harder for indecisive men to make a commitment to stay, it is also harder for them to make a commitment to leave!

The third point is that asymmetry of commitment is more common among couples who are living together rather than separately.

This fits with the idea of "inertia" or what other researchers have called "premature entanglement". Couples who move in together are more likely to find themselves stuck because one of them turns out to be less committed. Couples who haven't yet moved in together are more likely to discover the asymmetry of commitment and call it a day.

This should trigger yet another warning about the risks of moving in too soon.

If you move in together before you have a reasonably clear plan for where the relationship is going, you can end up stuck in a relationship that is going nowhere. When it does finally blow up, you can end up a lot more heartbroken than you might otherwise have been.

Sarah's story

My story is complicated. I have a deep longing for love and commitment. I thought I'd found it in Sam. He gave the appearance of being committed. Yet both of us brought "baggage" from our family upbringings. For Sam, it made it hard for him to sustain his commitment. My problem was that my love for him made me blind to its absence. Had I recognized the warning signs about his willingness to commit, I probably wouldn't have invited him to move in so soon. It was a mistake.

I think so much of it goes back to the relationship I have with my father. He was, and is, a kind man of integrity. He has a good heart and is deeply committed to Mum and me. But his own upbringing often makes him appear cold, stiff, and old-fashioned. My need for his acceptance clashes with my desire to be different to him. And so we had a fiery relationship as I grew up. I have never really felt fully accepted.

In my relationship with a man, I want that same reliable commitment, but I want it expressed with emotion, understanding, and acceptance. My problem is that when I find a man who expresses himself, I miss the signs that should warn me to check he's in for the long haul.

My first serious relationship was with a man who was wonderfully charming and loving. I would have married him in the blink of an eye if he'd asked. But the subject never came up. He left when Sean, our son, was two. I don't think the experience made me sceptical of men or relationships generally. I knew that he had his own family baggage that made him flighty and unwilling to settle. I make sure our son sees his father wherever possible.

Two years on from that I met Sam. I fell in love with him because he was so kind to me and to Sean. He recognized that if he wanted to make it work with me, we came as a package. I had a poor job that helped me make ends meet. He said he wanted to help me support Sean financially, which was sweet and helpful. I really loved him and I loved how he treated Sean. I thought these were good signs of commitment. So I invited him to move in with me.

A few months later, he stopped the payments. I didn't mind because he didn't have to do it in the first place. I was never entirely sure what he did for work anyway. When he did work, it was mostly casual labour, painting and decorating, serving in a bar, helping friends out. There was nothing dishonest. But it was increasingly clear that as well as being his lover, I was expected to be the breadwinner, cook, and cleaner. He was always kind, accepting, and understanding to both of us. I never voiced it, but I think he needed me to mother him.

It took four years with him for me to realize that I would never get the commitment and reliability I needed. He had explicitly told me he would never marry. His own family history had made him distrustful of commitment. I understood that. But eventually I stood my ground and told him he had to pull his weight. He left the next day. We're still friends and Sean misses him.

Could we have made it work if I'd been willing to put up with his lack of commitment and need to be mothered? I suppose so. But I'd only have been kidding myself that this could be reliable.

Could I have pulled out earlier? It's so hard because I loved him so much, and still do. My mistake was inviting him in too soon. I was blind and misread the signs. He wasn't moving in for us. He was doing it for himself.

It still hurts that we couldn't make it work. And I would have wondered what might have been if I'd never let it get going. If somebody I trusted had sat me down after a couple of years and made me face reality, maybe I would have acted earlier. I just don't know.

Asymmetric cohabitation: the new patriarchy?

Sarah's story is a good example of how society has changed both for better and for worse.

Up until about fifty years ago, there were fewer lone parents bringing up children on their own. Had a lone mother like Sarah met Sam then, moving in together would not have been a serious option. They would have taken time to make their fledgling relationship work, while they established whether or not it was going to lead to marriage.

Since Sam told her early on that it wasn't, even his charm and kindness would have been insufficient to persuade her that the relationship was ever going to be a starter. The fact that he struggled with commitment per se, and not just marriage, may never have come to the surface because the relationship would have ended.

Today, moving in together has almost become a universal presumption. Perhaps Sarah could have held off for longer on the basis that she had a son to worry about. Even then, it would have been hard for her to resist somebody who was clearly kind and putting his best foot forward.

But having won his prize of living with Sarah, Sam backed off and showed his true colours, by which time it was hard for Sarah to ask him to leave.

It then took four years for either of them to overcome the sheer inertia of cohabitation. That's a long time to hang around in a relationship that is going nowhere.

But there's a very specific problem that couples face in relationships where one person is more committed than the other.

The more committed partner cares more about the future of the relationship. They are therefore more willing to put their own interests to one side for the sake of the relationship and let things go.

The less committed partner, on the other hand, cares less about the future of the relationship. They are therefore less willing to forgo their own interests.

Whether the relationship succeeds or fails is therefore in the hands of the less committed partner. He or she has the power, the control.

I'm not sure what word we might use to describe this when it's the woman who has control. But I do know what we say when a man has control. It's called patriarchy.

It's one of the ironies of modern culture that we often think of marriage as being patriarchal. Yet asymmetric commitment is relatively rare among married couples. When you have two people with equal lifelong commitments – in theory at least – neither of them has more power over the other.

But what we find in the US studies – and are almost certainly seeing in the UK – is that asymmetric commitment is a lot more common among unmarried cohabiting couples. And in two out of three cases, it's the man who is less committed and who therefore holds the power.

Today, it is cohabitation – not marriage – where you are most likely to find patriarchy.

Do you love me?

Having said all that, whether male or female, this basic question needs answering.

Do you love me?

At time of writing, I have been married to my wife Kate for over thirty years. I know, I really know, I really, really know, that she loves me. And she knows, she really knows, she really, really knows, that I love her.

Somewhere along the way, between our first meeting at Greenwich and today, we have banished any doubts about this.

There is no longer any ambiguity whatsoever.

Somewhere along the way, we have also established that we have the same level of commitment to one another – symmetry rather than asymmetry – where both of us know we have the same intention, the same plan for a life together.

There is no asymmetry between us, nor any imbalance of power and control such that one of us cares less than the other and can pull the plug if it all becomes too much.

We have equality of commitment. How do you get to that?

CHAPTER 5

RULES FOR ROMANCE

Imagine you want to start a business.

You know you can't do it all on your own. So you need a business partner, somebody who can do some of the things that you can't do, or maybe don't have time or inclination for.

They need to be able to support, motivate, and complement you. They'll be the extra brain and pair of hands that you need, offering new ideas and sharpening your own.

Most of all, they'll need to be able to work well together with you as a team. That means you need to be able to trust them and get on well with them.

So when you start looking for a business partner, you will have in your mind some set of criteria that you are looking for. You may be lucky and chance upon somebody who is an absolutely perfect fit. But the odds are that you will have to make a choice from a limited pool of applicants and decide if that person fits enough of your criteria that you can both make it work.

Even when you do find someone suitable, you'll want to check them out by talking to people who have known them or worked with them. Only then do you

> invite them to work with you, initially on a trial basis for a period of time during which it is easy for either of you to walk away if it's not working.
>
> Choosing well is extremely important. And so it is with relationships.
>
> Choose well and you have the makings of a partnership where both of you can give each other the reliable love each of you needs, hopefully for the rest of your lives.
>
> Choose badly and you have a battle on your hands.

Rule 1: Is he or she marriageable?

"Dad, I've got a new boyfriend."

"That's wonderful darling. I'm thrilled for you."

"And guess what? He's marriageable."

This was an actual conversation with one of my daughters. And as you can imagine, it caused me to do an invisible fist pump.

Yes, I thought. Dad is not completely useless after all. She has paid attention to Dad's first rule of romance: choose somebody who is marriageable.

So why "marriageable" and what does it mean?

Well, let's start with what it doesn't mean!

I don't mean that you need to marry them straightaway or even at any point in the future. But, using the business partner analogy, if you are going to build a relationship with somebody that has the potential to last, you need to start with somebody with whom you could imagine there is at least some potential for a future together.

So that person needs to have sufficient positive characteristics that put them somewhere in the pool of potential prospects.

And since that also means you may want to be considering marriage at some point, they need to be "marriageable".

Unless you just want to have fun and no particular prospects, what you don't want is somebody who doesn't fit the bill, who you could never imagine marrying. If you can't see any kind of future with them, then you are wasting your time and probably setting yourself up for heartache.

In other words, you need to look for something a bit deeper than "Wow! They look amazing!"

Now I don't want to be too prescriptive about what "marriageable" means. I can easily imagine that one person might especially value some particular character trait over anything else. Whereas for another person, that character trait is less important than whether their potential partner can provide financial security.

I know that the current political and media narrative is to be sceptical of apparent differences between men and women. There's a really positive aspect to this in terms of aspiration and opportunity. As husband of an inspiring, dynamic, and capable wife – and as a father of four similarly inspiring, dynamic, and capable daughters, we have always talked about going for anything they set their mind to and not feeling limited or constrained by what other people think.

But there are some important differences between men and women in the world of how we relate. We've already looked at one such difference, where men's commitment tends to be more closely linked with the decision-making process.

Another such difference is in the way men and women respond to one another in relationships. And remember we're talking "on average" here. So it may be that your experience is quite the opposite.

A finding that frequently crops up in research studies is that while women are more sensitive to the way they are treated, men are more sensitive to the level of argument reached.

So, for example, Professor Scott Stanley and colleagues surveyed 908 adults who were in a relationship, whether engaged, married, or cohabiting. This sample was representative of the US population in terms of age, income, and experience of divorce.[1]

The men in the study were far more likely to report problems if they noted that they handled arguments badly as a couple (we'll discuss this more in the next chapter). They were also more likely than women to walk away from arguments.

In contrast, for the women, the positive aspects of life – the extent to which they felt satisfied with their relationship, their levels of friendship, fun, and sensuality – were just as important as the way they handled arguments badly.

Two studies by Professor Frank Fincham and colleagues of ninety-six couples in the US produce similar sorts of findings from a slightly different angle. They found that wives handled argument better if they received more forgiveness. Husbands handled arguments better only if the level of conflict was lower.[2]

These studies give us some useful pointers for how men and women might think slightly differently about what "marriageable" might mean.

- A "marriageable" man treats women well, doesn't walk away from difficult arguments, is able to forgive, and can be a friend.
- A "marriageable" woman deals well with conflict, without degenerating into bad behaviour.[3]

In the survey of 300 mothers that Kate and I ran for our book *What Mums Want and Dads Need To Know*, we asked mums to tell us how highly they rated each of twenty-nine roles, qualities, and characteristics in their husband or partner.

As I mentioned earlier, at the top of the list came being friends, being interested in them, being a co-parent, being interested in the children, being kind, and being forgiving.

At the bottom of the list came the ability to fix things, the ability to earn, and being adventurous.

The things at the bottom of the list weren't unimportant. They just weren't as important as friendship, interest, kindness, and forgiveness. Also high up the list were being encouraging, appreciative, helpful, and patient.

If I had to put one factor at the top of my list, based on my own experience of over thirty years of marriage, it would be kindness.

Kindness is an active word that means you've had to think about somebody and what they might need or appreciate. It shows that you are other-centred and not self-centred. Gentleness is part of kindness but is not active enough: you can be gentle through gritted teeth. But kindness means showing care, being considerate and thoughtful, and then doing something about it.

Most of us sit up and notice when we hear about some little random act of kindness. We think "How kind!" when somebody stops, or gives, or asks, or cooks, or tidies, or helps, or listens.

To me, a kind person is a "marriageable" person.

When Kate and I first met, she says she saw in me somebody who was decent, truthful and honourable, socially similar, and someone with whom she could see a future. Although I was introverted and not as actively thoughtful as she would have liked, I was still kind. Had I been loud and gregarious, the life and soul of the party, she could never have gone out with me. Instead my quiet reserve meant I could be trusted not to run off with someone else. For her, I was a safe bet.

What I saw in Kate when we first met was somebody who looked gorgeous and was kind. She was also fun, bubbly, and vivacious – all of the things that I wasn't. Our similar social backgrounds were definitely a plus but, for me, not essential. Nonetheless, I knew very early on that this was the girl I wanted to marry.

Although neither of us would have used the word "marriageable" back in the mid-1980s, without knowing it each of us had a framework of what "marriageable" meant in order to size each other up.

As things turned out, I am delighted to say that we both chose exceptionally well!

You can see that each of us had slightly different versions of what "marriageable" meant. But whatever it means to you, just having this word in your head will reduce the risk of wasting your time. You want somebody with whom you can imagine a future together.

Is he or she marriageable?

Rule 2A (for women only): Does he fight for you?

Sacrifice.

It's not a very fashionable word. But sacrifice is an essential ingredient of commitment, especially for men.

So this is a question for women to ask of men. Does he fight for you?

All of my four daughters have found this question very helpful. Worthy boyfriends have impressed with their willingness to go out of their way for them. Former boyfriends have fallen short!

Sacrifice means putting yourself out, doing something for somebody else that puts their interest above yours. It's the opposite of selfishness or self-centredness.

It should be self-evident that willingness to sacrifice is going to be good news, not just for commitment, but for the happiness of the relationship,

Sacrifice can mean little things, perhaps giving something up for the sake of the other.

For over thirty years – including the two years before we married – Kate and I have had a running joke about who eats the last chocolate in the box. We insist the other has it until eventually one of us strikes, to the faux dismay and outrage of the other. Secretly we're pleased when the other gets the treat.

Sacrifice can also mean doing something you'd probably rather not do in order to save the other person from having to do it. Household chores are a good example. No, leave the washing-up. I can do that.

Or it could involve a bit more effort. Here's a simple way I put myself out for Kate.

Kate's work as a cookery teacher used to involve running a lot of evening classes. That meant finishing late in the evening. Unless the weather was bad, most nights she would cycle home. But one night somebody accosted her outside our front door and tried to mug her. Although I ran out and chased him off, the whole episode really scared Kate. She stopped cycling. Every night from then on, I drove into town and collected her from her classroom.

You could call this love or duty or the right thing. But sacrifice is any of the little ways we put ourselves out for one another.

These might include doing a chore for the other, watching a TV show that the other wanted to watch, deciding not to buy something you really want, changing the way you say things, changing your timetable or plans, not complaining when the other is under pressure, listening when you're not interested.[4]

Part of the reason sacrifice is linked to commitment is that it requires a sense of future relationship.

When I do something for Kate, I'm not expecting anything in return. That's what sacrifice means. I'm not keeping score. There are no terms and conditions attached. It's not a contract. I'm not doing it so that I can build up a stock of brownie points.

Can you imagine the nightmare of keeping score?

You haven't paid me back for that lift I gave you to the office last week. I did the washing-up four times last week and you only did it three times. No, you didn't!

Keeping score quickly degenerates into cries of "It's not fair!"

Commitment necessarily includes sacrifice without expectation. When you both sacrifice for one another, then you both get the most from your relationship. It's a win-win.

We give to each other and look out for one another because we have a sense of a long-term future together.

So does he fight for you? Clearly I don't mean physically fight. I mean sacrifice, put himself out for you?

And why have I posed the question as one for women to ask, rather than men? Why shouldn't this be a question for men to ask too?

The simple answer is that men's willingness to sacrifice is a particularly good sign of their commitment. If a man gives up his time or resources to do something for you, it suggests that he is committed. Although committed women also show willingness to sacrifice, so do uncommitted women. So if a woman gives up her time or resources, it's just not as clear a signal of whether she is committed or not.

A couple of studies have investigated this phenomenon.

In one study that followed thirty-eight couples during the early years of their marriages, those who were happy making small sacrifices for one another were more likely to have better quality marriages a year or two later. But whereas happiness with sacrifice was independent of commitment for the women in the study, the two were closely related for the men.[5]

A second study of 145 married or cohabiting couples across a wide range of relationship duration looked at the opposite effect. Instead of investigating how happy couples were with sacrifice, they looked at how harmful couples perceived sacrifice to be to their own self-interest.

The results were much the same. Harmfulness was independent of commitment for women but closely (and inversely) related for men.[6]

What these studies reveal is that sacrifice is a big sign of commitment for men, but much less so for women. A committed man will be happy making sacrifices and doesn't consider them disadvantageous.

When I ask one of my daughters whether her boyfriend, or prospective boyfriend, fights for her, I am encouraging her to look for clear signs that he will put himself out for her.

Does he come over to her house, or does she have to do all the running?

Is he proactive in keeping in contact with her or does she have to keep the relationship going?

Does he occasionally offer to pay a reasonable bill for her, such as for drinks or the odd meal, or does he only ever insist that she pay her own way?

It may not be fashionable but is he kind and gentlemanly, in that he stands up for her, holds doors for her, and walks at her pace rather than charging on ahead of her?

A man who will do these things is showing the right kind of signs that he is willing to sacrifice his own interests, even if only in a minor way. It's not a guarantee that he can and will commit. But it's a good pointer. A man who doesn't do these things does not deserve her.

Does he fight for her?

There's clearly a lot of overlap here between willingness to make a decision and willingness to sacrifice – both of which qualities make men eminently marriageable. The difference is that "decision" is simply about making your mind up and doing something about it, whereas "sacrifice" is making your mind up and doing something that costs you.

Here's an amazing example of both in action.

Old friends of ours in Belgium are more or less trilingual. At home, they and their children all speak fluent French, which is their native tongue. But they also speak fluent Flemish, because it is the dominant language in the area in which they live, and fluent English, because it is an international language. It's incredibly impressive listening to the family flipping effortlessly from French to Flemish in a shop, for example, or into English when our family are staying. Of course, it's also slightly frustrating that their English is so good because I want to polish my French…

Anyway, one of their daughters began a relationship with a young man who spoke only Flemish. But he decided as part of his commitment to her that he would learn French so that he could communicate with her and her family in their native language.

This was an amazingly sweet and considerate act. It definitely shows a man who is capable of making decisions and a man who will put himself out for his girlfriend. It showed deep respect for her family but also sent a very clear and obvious signal of his commitment to her.

Rule 2B (for men only): Be that man!

Whether male or female, the way we treat one another and think about the future together is key for the success of any relationship.

A study of 252 men and women of a wide range of ages and relationship stages found that those who put a lot of thought into their relationship tended to do better across a range of outcomes.[7]

This should not be rocket science. It makes obvious sense that the more seriously you think about your relationship, the better you are likely to fare.

Having told my daughters that the key questions to ask of a man are "Is he marriageable?" and "Does he fight for you?", what do I tell my sons?

Simple. I tell them to be that man.

CHAPTER 6

ALL YOU NEED IS LOVE?

It's tempting to think that all you need is love. Yet the famous American relationship guru Professor John Gottman says that what puts a marriage at risk in its early years is not a lack of love; it's the way we treat one another negatively that matters most.[1]

In this chapter I want to look at some of the ways we react badly, almost without thinking. Invariably, these are rooted in our past experience and in particular the messages we have received about ourselves.

These bad habits – and the messages that drive them – are important because there is plenty of research to suggest that if you leave them unchecked, they can destroy a relationship.

Bad habits

Here's a question for you. What messages have you received through your life about yourself and how you perceive relationships? These could be messages from parents or teachers or some life event or even a previous relationship.

Some messages will be really uplifting: you can be anything you want to be; your parents are proud of you no matter what; you're deeply loved.

Others can be thoroughly destructive: you'll never make a success of anything; you're stupid; you're a loser.

All leave a mark that gives you some subconscious belief about yourself or others.

A dominant message for most of my own life was rooted in my experience of being sent to boarding school at age seven. I know my parents made the choice they felt was right at the time, so I have never judged them for sending me away from home so young. But I hated school as a result.

In order to deal with my sense of abandonment, I built a hard protective shell around me to keep the little seven-year-old boy inside safe. I decided from a very young age that it was better not to feel and better to make my way through life on my own. I'm not sure I ever voiced this and put it into words. But the very real consequences were that I became very independent and didn't always care what people thought of my actions.

It was only after Kate and I stood on the brink of divorce after the first eight years of marriage that I began to sort this out. (The full story of our descent to, and recovery from, the brink is in our aforementioned book *What Mums Want and Dads Need to Know*.)

Although for the next twenty-five years I was able to feel safe, loved, and accepted by my wife and children at home, I continued to wear the shell when I was around others. Whenever I felt threatened – rightly or wrongly – by friends or family in a discussion, I would become prickly and withdraw behind my shell. Only recently have I finally learned to deal with this.

All sorts of life experiences, especially during childhood when we are forming our view of the world, can cause people to react negatively and set up bad habits as adults.

We'll come back to what those bad habits look like shortly. But let's first hear the tragic story of a friend of ours who for too long carried the message that it is not safe to commit to somebody.

Judith's story

For me, John definitely exceeded the minimum rules for romance. He clearly loved me and treated me with care and consideration. As well as being very marriageable, he showed by his actions that he would go out of his way for me. But I was scared of marriage. Sometimes our family backgrounds conspire against us.

My childhood was idyllic.

My brother Robert and I were brought up on the suburban outskirts of a major city in the north of England. I always felt loved by my parents. They were not shy in showing their affection for each other or for us. They often hugged me and told me how much I was loved. They were always there for me, comforting me without hesitation or judgment when I needed support.

I never had to worry about being fed, picked up from school, or supported in my exams. The love I got from my parents was reliable.

We did a lot together as a unit. There were Christmas and birthday traditions, as well as shared family holidays in the summer, often at the same cottage deep in the English countryside. Mealtime with laughter was the centrepiece of everyday family life. Mum was a good home cook; Dad was funny. Sometimes they would overdo the affection, prompting Robert and I to roll our eyes at one another, "Oh Mum, Dad, do you have to?" Secretly I loved it. I loved their warmth and tenderness to one another. I felt safe.

Aged eighteen, I'd just finished my final school exams when we all sat down for what I assumed would be just another normal meal.

Dad spread his hands out on the table.

"Judith and Robert," he announced. I was expecting a joke.

"I've fallen in love with another woman. I'll be moving out this weekend."

Everything stopped. I never saw it coming. It was as if we'd just been in a car crash and my parents were both dead. I couldn't believe that all their years together, all the fondness and the love they had shown for one another, had been swept away, just like that.

Soon after Dad moved out, Mum told us that they had been having problems for many years. They'd tried to work it out, but their conversations, always away from us, had invariably broken down into bickering and argument. She had felt hurt and alone yet had somehow hidden it behind a sham of unity.

Even after deciding that they were going to separate, it was months before Mum found out that Dad had been seeing somebody else. Despite the shock, she said she was able to view it as a symptom of their problems, rather than the cause. But that was the end. Our dinner came a few days later.

Although Dad remarried, on the few occasions when I saw Mum and Dad together they seemed to get on as if nothing had happened. The pretence was weird.

I had three or four boyfriends in my twenties. But I knew none of them would last. I just couldn't see a future with any of them. Then I met John and fell in love.

He was kind and gentle to me. I loved him and knew he loved me. He even left his job and moved across the country to be with me. But I just couldn't ever shake that lingering uncertainty about whether he was the one. He asked me to marry him four times, I think. Each time, it was awful because it put me on the spot. But I couldn't say yes. The honest truth was that I was scared our marriage would end up like my parents' marriage. It was too big a risk to commit everything to John only to see it snatched away somewhere in the distant future for no good reason.

Not surprisingly, John eventually gave up on me. He'd waited four years for me to say yes and I couldn't. So he left. I was heartbroken, as was he.

I didn't see anyone for a few years after that. Now in my mid-thirties, I was increasingly thinking about children and marriage. So when Paul came along, I wanted to make it work. But the relationship was never quite what I'd hoped for. All too often perfectly ordinary conversations would suddenly degenerate into a nasty row. Whenever I asked him for anything, or even made a suggestion, he would accuse me of being critical and hard to please.

We drifted on for several years, in hope that things would improve. Part of me hoped he would ask me to marry him. Part of me knew it would be a giant mistake. It didn't matter because he never talked about it anyway.

On my fortieth birthday, I finally realized I'd blown my big chance. I should have married John. He had fought for me; he had proved it by moving jobs and asking me to marry him several times. I had loved him. He had been the one. Now it was too late.

I also realized that I'd never really given John a good answer each time I turned him down. I would mumble something about not being sure. But the truth was that I was scared. My parents' sudden break-up had shattered my trust in relationships. I was in a fog. Maybe if I'd been more honest, he might have tried one last time.

I told Paul it was over.

STOP signs

All of us have had painful childhood experiences, even if not as dramatic as mine or Judith's. The result is that we all have weaknesses that make us blow it at some point in our relationships. We also get tired or grumpy or irritated. We have a bad day at the office and we take it out at home. In short, we treat each other badly.

Why do we do this to somebody that we love?

Sometimes we can be trying really hard to make our relationship work when, out of the blue, some little thing will crop up and cause the most awful argument.

Everyone has arguments. Any time two people have differences, there's the potential for an argument. When people talk about compatibility, they are really talking about bigger differences. The more differences, the greater the potential for argument.

In surveys, people usually say that money is the number one thing they argue about.

But in fact, when couples become parents, what we mostly argue about is children – how to parent them, spend time with them, nurture them, and deal with their behaviour. Well behind this is how we manage chores, how we communicate, how we manage leisure time, and only then how we earn, spend, and save money.[2]

Yet although money may not be the most frequent topic of arguments, it tends to be the most stressful. Couples report that they argue for longer and with more intensity about money. These arguments are also the ones that are most likely to recur and least likely to be resolved.

But most arguments are not really about the subject itself. When we argue about money, for example, we're not really arguing about money itself. It's what money represents: our values, hopes, and fears, our willingness to trust and our need for control, our past and future, and our sense of identity: "I am somebody if I have money"; "I am in control with money"; "I can trust my loved one with money"; "I have a secure future if I have money"; "I fear losing money".

The way we discuss any of these issues really boils down to the way we argue. This in turn reflects these deeper issues of fear, power, control, and identity. When we realize this, it becomes more obvious that how we handle our differences is the key to a successful relationship.

So it's not the subject that matters so much. It's how we handle it.

What do these bad habits look like?

Based on work by two American research groups who identified the most negative behaviours, I came up with the idea of STOP signs: four little red flags that are easy to remember and which will hopefully also stop you in your tracks.[3]

The common factor behind all of these bad habits is our attitude and the messages that lie behind it.

S is for Scoring points

You are scoring points when your argument descends into tit for tat.

"You left your trousers on the floor, again."

"What? Well, you left the dishes in the sink. Again."

"OK, since we're getting it all out there now, you didn't book in the car like I asked you to. Nor did you post my letter."

"Well, you're not so perfect, are you?"

"If you don't like it, you're free to leave."

And so on.

Few people get out of bed deliberately thinking of ways to criticize or create conflict. This argument started with a complaint that was delivered badly and taken badly. A simple apology for leaving trousers lying around would have nipped this in the bud, thereby stopping an argument from escalating out of control and giving this couple a thoroughly unpleasant start to their day.

T is for Thinking the worst

You are thinking the worst when you stop taking things at face value and assume there's more to it than meets the eye.

Perhaps you're in trouble or they're out to get you: "He's bought me flowers. He never does that normally. What's he done wrong?" "He's being nice all of a sudden. I wonder what he wants?" "She made herself a cup of tea this morning, but didn't make me one. What have I done to upset her?"

Just as with scoring points, most people don't wake up in the morning with a hidden agenda that means they are out to get you. The usual reason why situations get misinterpreted is past experience. Maybe every time a teacher or parent spoke to you when you were a child, it was to criticize. Or maybe somebody treated you badly in a previous relationship. It's not surprising that, when faced with a similar comment, action, or tone, it triggers an old reaction that should no longer apply in new circumstances.

O is for Opting out

You are opting out when, at some point in an argument, it all becomes too much.

"Right, that's it," you say, getting up and leaving the room. The trouble is that walking away like this sends a message that you don't care. You don't want to deal with it. It's not important enough to you. You're no longer listening. You're blanking them.

Some people find conflict at home really hard to deal with. The stress of the argument becomes too much. That might be OK if you make things clear: "I'm not handling things very well at the moment. Give me a few minutes." Once you've calmed down, you can try again. The trouble is that most of us don't take time-outs, which are healthy, like this. We walk away and don't come back, closing the door on this topic. Make a habit of this and eventually so many doors are closed that there is no room for conversation and friendship. Not good.

P is for Putting down

You are putting down when you look down on somebody.

Somebody does something that winds you up. A white van nearly reverses into you. A parent mistreats her child in the shop. A telephone call-centre employee can't deal with your enquiry. Every bone in your body cries out "Moron!" You sigh in frustrated contempt. You roll your eyes. You utter the odd expletive.

This is all very well in situations that don't really matter. But don't do it at home. When you put somebody down, you are saying that they have less value than you. You are clever; they are stupid. Even if it's true, it's not a great way to run an intimate relationship between friends and lovers.

Dealing with STOP signs

I first came up with the idea of STOP signs because I wanted a simple way of explaining the four bad habits that destroy relationships. Over the years, I've taught this idea to thousands of couples and new parents. (If you want more detail, you can find it in my book *Let's Stick Together: The Relationship Book for New Parents*.[4])

By being honest about my own shortcomings, I found that most people could immediately spot their own STOP signs.

My own particular weaknesses were Opting out and Thinking the worst. Even as my marriage to Kate pulled out of its terrible nosedive and began to resemble something far happier, I knew I had an unfortunate tendency to assume I was in trouble with Kate unless shown otherwise.

When I was teaching this idea to a group of exhausted new mothers in a post-natal clinic, admitting my own shortcomings would come across as funny. Most of them could relate to it. Alas, at home it was little short of a plague on our marriage.

As an example, Kate might point to the overflowing bin in the kitchen and say, "The bin is full." Since we had six children, it was essential for us to share responsibilities. With so many things that needed doing, we had to work together as a team. Most of the time, we were really good at it. If Kate had her hands full with other things, it should have been a straightforward request for me to empty the bin.

Instead, what I heard was, "Harry, what were you thinking? Why haven't you emptied the bin yet? Now I'm cross with you. You're in trouble." Feeling under pressure, I would react in one of two ways. I would first empty the bin. But then either I'd find an excuse to head off to my office and hide, or I'd close down and stop talking. This was me Opting out – in effect retreating once again into my protective shell.

This kind of reaction could happen at any time. I knew it was ridiculous. I knew it wasn't real. I was aware of it. I taught about it regularly. And yet the voice in my head that said, "You're in trouble, Harry" never left.

That message was frustrating for me. But it was slowly driving Kate mad. She never quite knew how to ask me for something in case she said it wrong. Over the years, my unpredictable responses took their toll. Just like me, Kate's own version of Thinking the worst led her to Opt out.

Yes, it plagued our marriage.

The run-up to our daughter's wedding a few years ago multiplied this by a million. There'd been so much to organize in a short space of time, so many opportunities for Kate to ask me to do something. The result was that I spent much of the time feeling utterly closed. It wasn't healthy or positive. It put a big dent in my relationship with Kate.

Of course, the wedding itself brought this time of prickliness to an end. It was a truly magical day for all the family. But it also strengthened my own resolve to deal with my natural inclination to Think the worst and Opt out once and for all.

Weeks afterwards, we were relaxing on our summer holiday and I brought the subject up with Kate. Even if her muffled sigh told me the extent of her frustration and resignation, there was love in her eyes as she turned to me.

"But, Harry," she said, "you know I love you and want to be close to you."

I did. I really did know this. Kate had often told me how all she ever wanted was to be close to me.

For me, it was one of those light-bulb moments. I knew that this was the voice I needed to hear every time she looked at me, every time she shouted at me, every time she asked me to do something, every time she said anything at all.

It wasn't the way she said it that needed to change; it was the way I saw her. It was the voice I heard. It was the big picture. Kate wasn't out to get me. I wasn't in trouble. I had a wife who loved me and wanted to be close to me.

It was as simple as that and it has revolutionized our marriage.

Changing the message

Kate was inevitably sceptical that I would change. But I knew I could now hear a different message whenever Kate spoke. I'd found a way of squashing the voice that said "You're in trouble" and replacing it with a voice that said "I love you and want to be close to you."

I hope it's made me a kinder, more attentive husband. I am less fearful of being told off and hardly ever Think the worst now. I also no longer need to Opt out quite so much by spending more time than is strictly necessary in my office. I am now much freer to hang out with Kate wherever she happens to be in the house.

This has allowed Kate to be much more relaxed around me, no longer having to tread on eggshells or worrying whether she had said something the wrong way to me. It's brought softness, cherishing, and a deeper friendship.

It's also brought a renewed confidence to Kate. Over the years, she'd never really accepted that I was proud of her when I said it. She never believed it because I wasn't attentive. Now she can hear it.

Today we have learned to laugh off our little bad habits. We have a big-picture view of our marriage. We're in it for the long haul.

We say to ourselves, "Harry – or Kate – is just having a bad day at the office." We then attribute the grumpiness to some other factor. The big picture tells us that we are with somebody who is a good person who loves us. So any bad reactions must be due to something else, whether it's pressure at work, not feeling well, or being worried about something.

We still have to be careful not to attribute these odd bouts of bad behaviour to them as a person. It's not their circumstances; it's who they are. He or she is erratic, prickly, grumpy, unkind, bad-tempered. This thought process can easily become a slippery slope. We begin to lose sight of the big picture and get more and more focused on what's going wrong.[5]

But changing the message has made a huge difference to our marriage

What are your messages?

At the risk of getting too deep and meaningful about all this, we can usually find the roots of our bad habits laid down and buried somewhere in our past. We react badly towards our loved ones because of the way we were treated, the messages we were given, the way we see ourselves, the things we most need.

Our own story is a salutary lesson on how the effects of parenting – both good and bad – can be very long-lasting indeed. The way each of us was brought up as a child took us on into adulthood with certain messages in our minds.

Some of those messages have proved really positive and helped us as a functional couple. You are independent. You have freedom to choose. You can do whatever you want to do. You will always be OK.

Other messages have been negative and led to dysfunction. You're in trouble. You're always putting pressure on us. You're tricky.

It's really important that this is not used as an excuse to blame or criticize our parents. After all, just as few of us wake up in the morning with the intention of being horrible to one another, it's highly unlikely that any of our parents set out to be anything less than the best they could be in the circumstances.

Judith's story shows how destructive divorce can be when it comes out of the blue. In a low-conflict split, parents are often convinced that they are doing the best for all of the family. The trouble is that children see things from a completely different perspective.[6]

But even in some of the healthiest intact families, we can get the wrong messages.

Parents can love us in their own way, but somehow we don't feel loved in the way we need. Parents have high hopes for us, but we lack confidence in ourselves. Parents are proud of us, but we crave affirmation because they never really showed it.

We've often joked with our own children that we will pay for their counselling as adults! And we will, if that's what they want.

It took us nearly thirty years to identify a key message that undermined our marriage. Don't let that happen to you.

What are your STOP signs? And what are the messages that make you react in that way?

CHAPTER 7

TO MARRY OR NOT?

Having chosen well, the question I want to discuss now is whether you ought to get married or not.

Of course, in most normal circumstances, nobody is forced to get married. But it's worth asking why the odds of a successful relationship and thriving family life seem stacked so much more in your favour, and your children's favour, if you do.

My research at Marriage Foundation shows that between seven and eight out of ten married parents manage to stay together while bringing up their children. By way of comparison, only three out of ten unmarried parents stay together.[1]

A great deal is known about why, on the whole, marriage works. Couples who marry have made a mutual decision about their future together, they've made their plan crystal clear to one another, and their family and friends know all about their plan so can affirm them and support them.

Not much is known about why that three out of ten unmarried couples do so well. But I suspect they are doing most of the same things that successful marriages do and have done.

Whereas all of these good things happen automatically when couples get married, they require a very deliberate and considered strategy for couples who don't.

> So make it easier on yourselves and put the odds in your favour from the beginning! Get married before having children.
>
> What's not to like?

Deciding to succeed

About twenty years ago, I discovered I have a genetic problem called coeliac disease. Two other close relatives suffer from it so it seems to run in my family.

What this means is that gluten – found in wheat, barley, and rye – destroys the villi in my small intestines. Villi are little wiggly things that absorb vitamins. Pretty important, really. No villi, no vitamin absorption.

Until I found out and was properly diagnosed, I used to think I could eat whatever I wanted and never seem to put on weight. This was great! Yet without realizing it, I had been happily eating normal things like bread and pizza and pasta that were slowly poisoning me. This was why I was thin – gaunt even.

Having found out that my thinness was caused by my inadvertently poisoning myself, I looked at my overweight father and saw the future. With my diet changed, I realized that unless I changed my lifestyle substantially, there was a real risk of my following in his (considerable) footsteps! So I decided to get properly fit. I needed a goal to motivate and challenge me. I ran my first thirteen-mile half-marathon six months later.

Since then, I've done at least one half-marathon every year, usually in late summer. But in order to fight my tendency to get fit in summer and then revert to fat in winter, I've occasionally entered races in the spring, which force me to stay fit through the winter as well.

In 2018 I finally bit the bullet and decided to go for the full 26-mile marathon.

A full marathon is a whole different animal to a half-marathon. If you're not a runner, a half-marathon may still seem like a long way. But since its well within the ability of almost anyone to walk it, running it – even if stop–start – is an achievable step up from that for most people.

Nonetheless, I was apprehensive about doubling the distance and wasn't 100 per cent sure I could manage it within a sensible time.

After spending a bit of time online researching training plans, I decided to give it a go. A suitable race near where I live was due to take place in early April and I would start training on 1 January. So I had just over three months to work with. I didn't have to fill in the application for the race itself until a week beforehand. So I had an opt-out clause if it turned out to be beyond me. I set myself a series of mini goals that would tell me if I was on track.

My first mini goal was to lose a stone (a little over six kilos) in weight during January. I didn't fancy carrying the Christmas turkey on all of my training runs, let alone for a whole marathon. So I stopped drinking alcohol, ate smaller portions, stopped snacking, and duly lost a stone.

My next mini-goal was to be able to run my first practice half-marathon by mid-February. On a lovely quiet country road not too far from home, I gradually increased my distances each week and managed a thirteen-mile run once a week for the next four weeks.

Finally I intended to complete a twenty-mile run by mid-March, three weeks before the race itself. I managed that even though the last few miles were pretty horrible.

At that point, I decided I'd done enough to apply for the race. So I bit the bullet, filled in the form, sent in the money, and set up a fundraising web page.

I then did one other thing that really sealed the deal. I sent out an email to all my friends asking for sponsorship.

Until that moment, my plan to run a marathon had been private. Only my immediate family knew of my plan. They were very supportive. But I had an exit route. I knew I could back out at any point without too much loss of face.

However, once I'd made it public and told all my friends, then I knew I was truly committed. I was all in.

And so, in early April, I set off for my first marathon.

I stuck to my game plan of getting past the first sixteen miles at my usual pace and then taking it a mile at a time. Somehow I kept going and going. The miles ticked by. For the last four miles one of my sons and a couple of friends ran with me. It was great having them but I ended up worrying whether they were OK. After all, I was in a groove and they were coming in from cold.

Anyway, I finally got to the finish line and was thrilled to complete the marathon in just under my target time of four hours. It felt easier than I had feared. But completing the race was built on my initial decision to give it a go, the advice I found on online blogs, the trust I had in my training plan, the way I could tick off my mini-goals as I achieved them, and my determination to stick at it.

In the end it was my decision to sign on the dotted line and tell all my friends that cemented my commitment to running my first (and possibly only) marathon.

Does this process remind you of anything?

The evidence in favour of marriage

Nobody goes into a relationship wanting it to end. Everybody wants reliable love. But the fact is that married couples tend to stay together whereas unmarried couples don't. Staying together is the norm if you're married. It's the exception if you're not.

Clearly you don't have to get married to make a relationship work. But the odds are stacked against you if you don't.

One of the many studies we've done at Marriage Foundation looked at a group of 1,783 UK mothers with teenage children, all of whom had been living with the father as a couple when their baby was born. From the answers in the survey – called Understanding Society – we could track back to whether the parents got married before or after giving birth or never married at all.[2]

Nearly eight out of ten mothers who had married before they gave birth were still living together with the father, compared with just three out of ten mothers who had never married.

So being married before you have a baby seems to make a big difference to your odds of staying together. And this is not just because more of the married parents are staying together for the sake of the children. This might be true in some cases but it's not the main reason. Marriage influences stability – independently of relationship happiness.

But the unexpected finding was that fewer than half of the mothers who married at some stage after they had children were still together with the father. Getting married afterwards gives couples a bit of an advantage over couples who don't marry, but not as much as you might think.

Hold that thought and I'll come back to it shortly…

We were able to show that these huge differences in odds between those who married and those who didn't remained even when we took into account the mother's age or education. It could have been that women who were older or had a university degree were more likely to marry and it was these factors, not being married, which made the difference. They weren't.

We've also followed, for the Millennium Cohort Study, a much larger group of 18,000 UK parents whose children were born in the year 2000 or 2001. In all of our analyses, we've shown that parents who were married before their child was born were more likely to have stayed together through to their children's teenage years compared with parents who were cohabiting but not married.[3]

One of the usual criticisms of this kind of research is that it's not marriage that makes the difference. It's merely that the type of people who marry are quite different to those who cohabit. It's true that there are important differences in background between the two groups, such as age or education or ethnicity. But even when we take these into account and compare like with like, the married group still do better.

Some then insist that this is still not marriage but the quality of the relationship that is the important factor. In our studies, we also take into account how happy couples are with their relationship on the upside and whether they have ever experienced physical abuse on the downside. Married parents still do better.

Not only are they more likely to stay together, their teenagers' well-being also benefits from having two parents still around and from having a good relationship with the opposite sex parent – which is more likely to happen if both parents are still living in the same house.[4]

Deciding on a life together

Please bear with me as I revisit my running analogy – briefly, I promise!

At the end of 2018 I thought I might have another go at doing another marathon the following April.

I applied much the same principles as I had first time round. My first mini-goal was to lose the Christmas turkey by the end of January. My initial training runs were similar.

Alas, by the end of January I'd struggled to get down to my target weight. I'd gone dry and stopped alcohol as I did before. But I just hadn't been as disciplined about my food consumption. So my plan for a second full marathon was now been quietly dropped and I would stick to the much more achievable half-marathon.

The big difference was in my mindset. I was less determined and more indifferent about the whole thing. Yes, it would be quite nice to complete another marathon. But "it would be quite nice" is not the same as "I'm really going to do this."

And that is the major difference between deciding and sliding and one of the key reasons why stable marriage is the norm whereas stable cohabitation is the exception.

The key decision made by couples who get married happens long before the ceremony. It's the conversation they have when they decide and agree to spend the rest of their lives together.

"Will you spend the rest of your life with me?"

"Yes."

That engagement conversation is the moment that brings together lots of the good things we talked about when we discussed dedication.

- It sends a signal. It gives each partner important information about their mutual commitment to one another.
- It brings clarity. It should now be completely obvious to both partners what their plan is. They want to spend the rest of their lives together. That's the plan.
- It removes ambiguity. Any worries that he or she might not be as committed as you can now be banished.
- It brings equality. With both partners showing equal commitment, there is no more asymmetry that allows the less committed partner to hold the more committed partner to ransom.

But the key action that cements this commitment is the ceremony itself.

I remember vividly the morning of my own wedding day back in 1986. It was the most gorgeous warm sunny day, the kind of classic English summer's day in June, for which the word "quintessential" was invented.

And yet I had the worst attack of butterflies that I can ever remember. I'd been in all sorts of hair-raising situations in my career as a Royal Navy pilot. I'd watched artillery shells explode around me in the middle of a war. But nothing before, or since, has come close to the nerves I felt in anticipation of my wedding later that day.

But as soon as I gathered with friends and family and waited for Kate to walk up the aisle, my nerves vanished. I had chosen well.

It may not be intuitively obvious why the ceremony should have any impact on the subsequent relationship. And yet it does appear to matter.

Two American studies have looked at a variety of factors involving the wedding and run up to the wedding. The most comprehensive is by economists Andrew Francis-Tan and Hugh Mialon, who studied 3,000 couples who either were married or who had been at some point.[5]

They found that spending a huge amount of money on the wedding was not especially helpful. In fact, the general rule was that the more money you spent, the higher the risk of divorce. Couples who spent less than £800 ($1,000) on their wedding did particularly well. Couples who spent more than £15,000 ($20,000) did particularly badly. Those who spent anywhere within this reasonably broad range had similar outcomes. Of course, this is all on average and there will be exceptions.

Those who bought a modest engagement ring costing somewhere between £400 ($500) and £1,500 ($2,000) also did well. Those who spent less or more did less well.

But the key point was that the more people who came to your wedding the better. Couples who eloped on their own or got married in front of fewer than ten people had the highest divorce risk, especially in the earliest years. Those who married in front of a lot of people did especially well.

One other American study of 418 newlyweds – where the average wedding size was 118 guests – reached much the same conclusion. The more people at the wedding ceremony, the happier the subsequent marriage.[6]

Remember that, in both of these studies, this is not about the cost of the wedding reception afterwards. It's about how many people come along to witness the ceremony.

Why might that make a difference? Well, for the same reason it helped diffuse my nerves.

Making a commitment to spend your life with just one person also means making a commitment to reject all of the other possibilities. It's making a choice to reject all other choices except one. As I attest, that can feel like a huge risk.

What having all of those people there does for you is give you a massive vote of confidence.

"Great choice, Harry. You've chosen well. You've done the right thing."

Using the garden analogy once more, they are increasing the size of the wall around the garden. That increases constraints that make it harder to leave – we're watching you, Harry!

But it also increases dedication – we're with you, Harry!

And so you can begin married life with the confidence that you've made a great choice and made a commitment in front of all your friends and family.

Do you have to marry?

Of course, you don't have to get married to make a success of your relationship. But if you choose not to, it's worth remembering the following things.

First, recognize that the odds are not stacked in your favour.

Nearly eight out of ten parents who are married when their baby is born will still be together when the kids finish school. In sharp contrast, only three out of ten parents who don't marry remain together.

Yes, there are plenty of success stories among unmarried couples. But they are the exception and not the rule.

Second, beware that in the UK at least there is no such thing as common-law marriage, and never has been.

If the worst ever did come to the worst and you split up, neither of you have any legal rights or responsibilities regarding your partner. You do to your children, but not to each other. Much the same is true if one of you dies.

If you're fine with that, then... fine!

Third, if you want to be in the successful minority of unmarried couples, then you need to make really sure you have done the things that make relationships work.

- Have you had a really clear and open conversation with your partner about your future together?
- Do you know for sure that both of you are committed to spending a life together?
- Are there any signals that show your mutual commitment to one another, beyond living together and having children – both of which can happen through sliding, rather than deciding?
- And have you told your friends and family about your plan? Remember: the commitment I made to my marathon only became concrete when I asked my friends for sponsorship. Having friends and family who are on your side – as a couple – gives you tremendous support but also makes you accountable: a little bit of pressure on you to make it work may be the motivation you need when the going gets tough, as it always will at some point in a relationship.

Or you could simply bite the bullet and get married.

Whatever you do, make a plan and do it for yourselves!

I asked you to hold a thought a few pages back. It was because of a seemingly odd finding that those who get married after having a baby don't seem to do much better than those who never marry at all.

In other words, marriage after you become parents doesn't seem to produce anywhere near the same level of stability as marriage before you become parents.

Why?

Well, even though I can't be 100 per cent sure about my answer, I'm pretty confident that I have a good explanation for this phenomenon. It's speculative but I think it makes sense.

The difference is between deciders and sliders; planners and non-planners.

Those who marry before having children are likely to be making their commitment to each other. Only then do they have children. Marriage is part of their plan. Children are also part of their plan.

One of the studies we did at Marriage Foundation looked at the previously mentioned Millennium Cohort Study of over 18,000 UK parents who had babies in the years 2000 or 2001. We compared couples who planned their child's birth with couples for whom the birth was a surprise.[7]

In a nutshell, parents who were married were more likely to be planners – 73% of married parents compared with 47% of cohabiting couples.

Whether married or not, planners tended to be happier with their relationship soon after their baby was born – both mums and dads were 10–20% more likely to report high levels of happiness and 30–35% less likely to report low to medium levels of happiness.

And couples were more likely to stay together if they were planners – by the time their child was aged three, only 8% of planners had split up, compared with 31% of the surprised group; by age fourteen, 24% of planners had split up compared with 45% of the surprised group. Married parents who didn't plan were 30% more likely to split; cohabiting parents who didn't plan were 24% more likely to split.

A big clue as to what's going on comes from the way UK divorce rates have been falling for the past two decades.

So yes, it's true. Contrary to what many assume, today's marriages now look more stable than at any time since the early 1970s. (Remember, we are talking about *rate* not number here – so this is not just because there are fewer weddings.)

My database at Marriage Foundation uses data from the Office for National Statistics to track divorce rates in England and Wales for every year of marriage. My own wedding year, 1986, turns out to have the highest divorce rates of any year ever!

However, for couples who have married in the years since 1986, we are seeing a big fall in divorces instigated by wives – though not by husbands – almost entirely during the early years of marriage. In fact, 80% of the entire fall in divorce rates can be attributed in this way.[8]

What I think is going on is that social pressure to marry has largely disappeared. You hardly ever hear people asking couples "When are you going to tie the knot?" or "When are you going to make an honest woman of her?" or other such patronizing questions! Yet in the days when almost every couple married, these sorts of challenges were normal and accepted. No longer.

Without that social pressure to marry, fewer of those who do marry will have only done so because they feel they have to marry. More will have married because they want to marry.

We've seen that deciding is especially important for men's commitment. Well, here's some further compelling evidence to support that. Marriages are more stable as fewer wives file for divorce. Unless women have become increasingly tolerant of men's bad behaviour – which seems highly implausible – the most likely explanation is that men who do choose to marry are more committed.

What we have are fewer sliders and more deciders.

And this is exactly what I think is going on among those who marry after their child is born. More of them – by no means all – are reacting to social or family pressure to get married for the sake of the children.

What they are not doing is getting married because they really want to make that commitment to one another. So they are *sliding* into marriage.

So, whether you get married or not, make a plan for your future together as a couple and commit to that plan. But do it for yourselves, because you want to do it and not because you have to do it, or because you're doing it for the kids.

CHAPTER 8

THE TWO-YEAR RULE

I've talked a lot about how couples in a less than perfect relationship can end up stuck together.

Whether it's called "inertia" or "constraints", the sheer complexity of living a life under one roof, the sunk costs of time, money, and effort that have already gone into your relationship, the aversion to losing what you have, and the difficulty of finding somewhere – or someone – else, all make it easier to stick with a less than satisfactory relationship than split up.

Drifting is easy. Breaking up is hard.

So couples get stuck or drift or slide, because they have never established a plan or each other's intentions. They've never had the talk, what Americans sometimes call "DTR" – Define the Relationship.

Of course, this feels risky because it might reveal the unpleasant truth that you or your partner aren't ready to commit – which in effect means won't commit.

So how long should you wait to have this conversation? Wait too long and you risk a perfectly good relationship going sour, struggling in a world of uncertainties, lingering doubts, and ambiguity.

Is there a sensible time to have this conversation?

Of course there is. It's the two-year rule!

Can you relate to any of these?

… I love him and know I could easily spend the rest of my life with him. We have a fun time together and he always treats me with kindness and consideration. But most of the time our life seems centred around now. Very occasionally we raise the subject of a future together beyond the next few weeks. But any discussion usually ends in nervous laughter and we change the subject. I think he is into me as much as I am into him. But I just have that nagging uncertainty in the back of my head. I'm scared of bringing the subject up, but I need to know where we are going with this. I need him to make his intentions clear.

… I love her and enjoy our time together. But to be honest, I just don't think very much about spending a life together. I'd like to get married one day. Our relationship is good for now but I'm not sure I'm ready for commitment yet.

… I love him and mostly enjoy where we are now. I don't know if he is the one but I'm not sure I've ever met anyone else who could be better. I think lack of certainty holds both of us back. I've caught myself being more snappy with him recently. That doesn't exactly endear him to me. We've felt close before and I think we could be close again if I knew we were going to spend the rest of our lives together. But I feel stuck and insecure. It seems like such a waste to throw a perfectly adequate relationship away. I'm still here because I don't have enough reason to leave. Yet I need something more if I'm to stay and build a family together.

Fear of loss

At some stage, all of these couples need to sit down, have a serious conversation about where their relationship is going, and make a decision one way or another.

They should commit or quit.

The trouble is that it's risky to have that conversation. What if it triggers him or her to say they've had enough and then for them to walk out? Fear of losing what you have prevents you from raising the subject.

Economists call this fear "loss aversion". This means we're more scared of losing what we have than excited we might gain something we don't have yet. For example, people are generally more willing to gamble on the possibility of winning £100 that they don't have than on losing £100 that they do.

This is similar to the idea of a "sunk cost". This means we'd rather keep going on a lost cause, because of the time or money or effort we've already invested, than give up and start again.

For example, we have a fireplace in our house. Last night I lit a fire in my usual way, with plenty of tinder, kindling, and fuel. Alas, I seemed to have used flame-proof wood! So as the fledgling fire died to an ember, I wondered whether I should put my efforts into fanning the feeble remains into flame or give up, clear it all away, start again, and build a new fire. Of course, I then spent far too long trying to resuscitate the dying embers by blowing madly on them, because I didn't want to give up. Eventually I saw the light and built a new fire that actually worked…

Relationships that drift on without any obvious end point are like that fire. You can expend a great deal of energy trying to fan them back into flames. In the end, you need to clarify whether that relationship has the potential to fire up again, or whether you are better off cutting your losses and starting again elsewhere.

In your relationship, having a serious conversation about the future will tell you whether or not there is real hope and whether or not you should persevere. Hopefully it will bring clarity, remove ambiguity, send a signal, and allow friends and family to affirm and support you in your plan.

But it also poses a huge risk that you might not get the answer you want.

How long should I wait?

So you've been together a couple of years. You have some questions that need answering – about whether this is the right relationship, or about whether your partner is as committed as you are. Perhaps you're worried that he or she will leave if you push them too hard.

Maybe if you hang around for a little longer, things will become clearer?

There are two reasons why more time isn't likely to help. The first is to do with information. The second is to do with odds.

First of all, it is clearly important to gather as much information as possible before making a commitment. Because making a commitment is risky, the longer you stay together as a couple, in theory the more information you have from which you can make your decision.

The logical conclusion from this is that you should never commit. Since there is always more to learn, you should wait... and wait... and wait!

However, research in other fields suggests that there comes a point where further information doesn't actually help you make better decisions. It might make you feel more confident about your decision. But it doesn't make the decision any more accurate.

This finding goes way back to a study conducted in the 1970s where punters were asked to predict the results of a horse race, based on increasing amounts of information about each horse. The extra information did nothing for the gamblers' success rate but made them feel a whole lot more confident about their predictions.[1]

More recent experiments involve university students who were asked to predict the results of soccer games, once again given an increasing amount of statistical information of the kind sports fans love. However, the accuracy of those predictions remained fairly consistent despite the addition of lots more statistics. What those statistics did increase was, once again, confidence in the predictions.[2]

Furthermore, you might think that discussing the weekend's sports with a friend ought to increase the amount of information or knowledge available about those games. Yet although it increases confidence in the results predicted, it also does nothing for accuracy.[3]

The second argument for why more time won't help is all about odds.

Along with my colleague Professor Steve McKay at the University of Lincoln, I took a look at what happened to some 25,000 UK unmarried cohabitees who took part in the British Household Panel Survey at some point between the years 1980 and 2000.

After each year of the survey, some couples went on to split up and some went on to get married, leaving behind those who were still together for the following year's survey. And of course, some couples dropped out of the survey so we don't know what happened to them. This is pretty normal in surveys and it's called attrition.

However, this gave us enough information to work out what proportion of couples made their relationship work, depending on whether they remained unmarried or got married.

Our first finding was that regardless of how long couples had lived together – whether we were looking at a group of couples who had been together for just one year, or a group that had been together for two years, or up to ten years – four out of ten couples were going to split up and not get married over the next decade.

So there doesn't appear to be any advantage – on average – of living together for longer in order to improve your odds of success. Couples who have lived together for a year have the same chance of splitting up as couples who have lived together for five years or ten years.

But of course some couples also get married along the way.

Among those who have lived together for just one year, we can say that five out of ten couples will marry at some point during the next decade – in addition to the four out of ten who will split up.

If we then look at a group of couples who have lived together for two years, or three years, that chance of getting married starts to reduce below five out of ten. By the time we look at the group of couples who have lived together for ten years, just three out of ten will subsequently get married.

Overall, what we can conclude from this is that no matter how long you live together, your chances of splitting up remain much the same – four in ten. But the longer you live together, your chances of getting married get smaller and smaller – reducing from five out of ten early on down to three out of ten.

So if you are a cohabiting couple, this is your future. Nine out of ten of you will either split up or get married.

But if you think you are quite happy as you are and don't plan to get married, your odds of achieving long-term stability is one in ten.

I think you will agree those are pretty poor odds.

For our second analysis, we wanted to do a direct comparison of whether it was better to stay unmarried or better to marry.

So let's imagine you have lived together for a while –what are your chances of staying together, whether you marry or not?

Starting with couples who had already been together a year, 75% of those who married were still together ten years later compared with 23% of those who didn't marry.

For couples who had already been together for longer, those chances improved.

Let's say we're looking at couples who have lived together for three years: their odds of success improved to 86% if they got married and 27% if they didn't.

By the time we look at couples who have already been together ten years, more than 90% of those who married survived the next ten years compared with only 42% of those who didn't marry.

The simple reason why the odds of success improve with every year – married or not – is that some of the more fragile couples have already split up along the way. As every year passes, we are looking at a stronger and stronger group of couples.

Yet even then, those who marry are still three times as likely to stay together compared with those who don't. Whereas staying together is very much the norm for couples who marry, it's the exception for couples who don't marry.

So if you want to stay together in your relationship, your chance of success is much better if you get married at some stage. However, beware that the longer you wait, the smaller your chance of getting married at all gets with every passing year.

The two-year rule

Given that most people want reliable love, and you will only find that reliable love when you make a mutual commitment to one another, there must be some appropriate period of time after which you have sufficient information to make your decision.

As part of my research for this book, I set up a simple online survey about the timing of various aspects of commitment.

I asked about when couples should sleep together, move in together, have a serious conversation about a long-term future together, make a proposal of marriage, and finally get married.

As I expected, there was a great deal of variation in views, especially about when couples should move in and whether they should get married. But what I was really interested in was whether people thought there was an optimum or maximum time by which couples should have been talking seriously about their future.

Almost all of the 317 respondents to the survey thought that there were both.

Only a handful of people thought this discussion about the future was "not important". The overwhelming majority – 88% – thought it was "very important".

In terms of timing, 89% of those who agreed there was an *optimum* time said it should happen within two years; 83% of those who agreed there was a *maximum* time said it should happen: within three years.

There were almost no differences in the way men and women answered these questions. Nor, perhaps surprisingly, was there much of a difference between those who thought marriage was important and those who did not.

There were also few, if any, differences between these groups in terms of what people actually did, rather than what they thought others should do. Across all groups, around eight out of ten had had a serious conversation about their own long-term future within two years. Nine out of ten had had their conversations within three years.

In so far as my survey reflects public opinion, it seems pretty clear that almost everybody thinks couples should have their big discussion about the future ideally within two years and certainly within three years.

And that is the two-year rule!

Commit or quit!

So let's bring together all of the information we've looked at in this chapter.

In order to build a relationship that is going to give you the reliable love you need and want for the rest of your life, you need to begin with a period of time spent gathering information; in getting to know each other.

But there will come a point where you have enough information to make that decision. Waiting longer won't tell you much more that you don't already know.

Waiting longer also keeps you in the high-risk cohabiting camp rather than moving to the low-risk married camp. The sooner you can move to the latter camp the better.

The 317 people we surveyed overwhelmingly suggested you need to have had that conversation about your future ideally within two years and definitely within three years.

After two years, you're not going to learn a whole lot more that you didn't already know about each other.

So after two years, it's time to commit or quit.

And that is why the two-year rule is a good one!

CHAPTER 9

COMMIT OR QUIT!

I think a lot of older couples have lost confidence in their ability to give wise advice to younger couples. They know that couples want reliable love. They know the way they did it themselves, which was to get married and have children in that order. But they've been worn down by the drip-drip of politicians, media, and Hollywood saying marriage doesn't matter so long as you're committed. Well, up to a point.

I hope in this book I've been able to give you some of your confidence back. Social norms may change but human nature doesn't.

But when you are faced with a couple you know and love who look like they are drifting on aimlessly, do you have any right to question or challenge them, or just mildly check out the way they choose to live their lives?

Provided you do it with love and kindness, and with a big smile on your face, of course you do!

Having the courage to encourage

Over the years, Kate and I have come across all sorts of friends or colleagues or adult children of friends who have been together for a while as couples. We have no hesitation about gently challenging them if it seems appropriate.

"Why don't you get married?"

"Why don't you ask her?"

"Why don't you tell him?"

"When are you going to get married?"

I remember Kate talking to a younger work colleague who had been going out with her boyfriend for several years. "When do you think you'll get married?" asked Kate. "Oh, we don't need to get married," she replied. "Why ever not?" asked Kate. "He doesn't want to." Aha. So he wouldn't commit to her. "So why are you with him?"

Recently, I was sitting next to a complete stranger at a conference. She asked about what I did. Within minutes, she then told me about her own relationship with her boyfriend and how long they had been together. I told her the two key questions I ask my daughters. "Is he marriageable? Does he fight for you?" I could see the cogs whirring in her head. Men need to decide in order to commit. Everybody gets it.

But what about when you know somebody well? What about your son or daughter? They've been together for a while and you think you ought to say something.

Here are two real stories to finish, with some of the background details blurred for anonymity, of two young couples who needed just the most gentle of prods. In both cases, the relationships were drifting. They weren't in trouble. But they needed a prod either to commit or quit.

In one case it was a prod from Dad. In the other it was a prod from Mum.

The consequences in each case have been that uncertain relationships have been converted into marriage. In each case the relationship has benefited hugely because of the resulting clarity and security.

I hope these stories will help give you the courage to encourage!

Seb's story

Louisa and I were childhood sweethearts. After completing university, we finally moved in together. But two years on, I was coasting and not really ready for marriage just yet. I barely noticed that Louisa had almost given up hope on me. I could have lost her. It was a couple of conversations with Dad that reminded me I needed to act.

We met in class because we were put next to each other. I think I'd been moved for being a bit too chatty. I liked her immediately. She was fun and kind and I wanted to spend time with her. It was more for my benefit at first but, over time, I soon realized that I wanted to do whatever it took to make her happy. I think she saw in me a good friend – someone she liked being around, someone who was loyal and kind, hopefully a decent human being.

But we're also very different. Whereas Louisa is extremely organized and likes to know what's going on, I'm much more relaxed and am happy to watch the world go by without worrying where I need to be going. On a recent holiday, for example, I just wanted to rock up and find somewhere to stay when we arrived. She needed every night booked in advance so she knew what was coming.

I can see it was pretty frustrating for her that when we finished university and moved in together, she wanted the next step – but it wasn't forthcoming.

She told me recently that she went along with almost anything I wanted to do, whether it was a night out or a weekend away, because she wanted to give me the opportunity to propose and not ruin my plan if she backed out. I never realized.

I was coasting, quite happy with life. We both had jobs. I could see our future together but I just wasn't ready to be a grown-up married man. I wasn't putting it off, but I certainly wasn't going out of my way to make a firm commitment to her.

Luckily, my parents are pretty wise. They could see Louisa needed the reassurance from me. I think I sensed that they wanted to say something and was expert at making sure we talked about other things.

Eventually Dad pinned me down on a car journey. I couldn't escape. He was very good about it. He just said right, you need to make a decision. You've been together for a couple of years. Don't leave her in limbo. Mum and I are concerned that she might not wait for you. So what's the plan?

We had a similar conversation a couple of weeks later. I told him I knew we'd be married in ten years, but not when. He said he knew I'd been putting it off but needed to act one way or another. Commit or quit.

Yes, I felt pushed, but it was what I needed. I knew his intentions were good. I needed to do something. It felt good to have to act.

By the time I did act, she had given up hope that I ever would. She looked shocked and said nothing for about two minutes. Then her face beamed with a huge smile. She was thrilled.

I'm not sure I noticed much of a difference in our relationship after we got engaged. I had always thought our relationship was good. But Louisa definitely did. She said she had felt increasingly on edge waiting for my proposal that never seemed to come. As a planner, being engaged made her feel a whole lot more secure. Now she had a plan.

We've been married for five years now and I love it.

John's story

Emma and I are similar to Seb and Louisa in some ways. We're in our mid-twenties and about to get married. We met just after leaving school so have known each other for several years. The difference is that I always wanted to get married but was putting it off – not because I didn't want to wait too long but because I wanted to wait for the right time. I just didn't know when that time was. A gentle prod from my mum and some warm encouragement from Emma's family helped me realize it was the right time.

It was early summer and I'd just finished my last exams at school. I was eighteen, young, free, and single. It was time to celebrate.

At one of many subsequent parties, I found myself standing next to Emma. She'd also just finished her exams. She had had a boyfriend for the past two years but their relationship was definitely drifting.

The chemistry between us was immediate. I fancied her and she fancied me. Fuelled by alcohol and the dizzy exhilaration of finishing school, we flirted with one another for a couple of hours before sneaking away from the party and off to my house. With my parents away, we spent our first night together.

Although we hardly saw each other during the next few months, we spent hours on the phone chatting and getting to know one another.

We moved into a flat-share together as we entered the world of work. After two years at drama school, I got a technical job with a theatre production company. Emma found work with a film company that was initially menial. But with a foot in the door, she soon took advantage of the opportunity to help with script development.

With work to keep both of us occupied during the days and enough money to have fun together in the evenings and at weekends, our relationship deepened. Soon after I got my first job, the subject of marriage began to crop up in conversation occasionally, jokingly referred to as the "M-word". It seemed to both of us that this was where we were headed. There was a real sense of future together.

I was well aware that I wanted to marry Emma. She was the one for me. But even five years into our relationship, we were both still only twenty-four years old. I was aware that sceptical questions were asked of older couples in their thirties. Were they going to get married? Why hasn't he asked her yet? I didn't want to get into that situation. But with the average couple getting married at around thirty, how long should I wait before asking?

Emma loved the way I joked about the M-word. It seemed to make her feel safe. I knew it was just a matter of time before I asked her for real. But after five years together, tiny seeds of doubt were beginning to creep in. We had stopped talking about the future, as if our future together were assumed. Is this what I wanted?

It was during arguments that the uncertainties flared into life. Our rows were never big. They were more like little spats. But in the uneasy peace that followed a row, Emma needed reassurance more than anything. She needed to know deep down that her future with me was secure, that we could have little miscommunications, that it was normal and OK, that it didn't threaten our relationship. I'm not sure I read the signs very well.

To my mind, the little rows did make me question whether Emma really was the one for me. I would tell myself that my adult life had barely begun, during which I'd only ever really known Emma. There were plenty of other fish in the sea. There was still the faintest possibility that I might not end up marrying her.

But my doubts were only ever fleeting. As soon as the next morning dawned, I would realize once more how lucky I was. I felt it. I just didn't tell Emma.

So how long should I wait before asking her? Two conversations were especially helpful to me.

The first came during a visit to Emma's family. Her brother took me to one side.

"Mate," he said. "All of us think you two are brilliant for each other. So if you did decide to make it permanent, we'd be absolutely thrilled."

The second was from my mother during a trip home on my own.

"Darling John," she said. "You've been with Emma for quite a few years now and, if you haven't done it already, I really think you ought to make your intentions clear to her. I've got a friend who has just been broken up with after fifteen years. She was waiting for him to marry her before she had children. I don't think you can do that to a woman."

It was the first time it had occurred to me that Emma might be thinking in that way. Her body clock was ticking. Yet all I was thinking about was what others might think: on the one hand, whether we were old enough; on the other, whether we had waited too long.

I proposed shortly afterwards.

Emma told me that being engaged made her feel deeply secure in a way she hadn't quite felt before. She hadn't felt particularly insecure beforehand. But any lingering doubts about our future, any tiny discomfort she might have felt at discussing marriage or children, had all disappeared.

The decision to marry felt very right to me. I'm not sure it changed a lot for me. Being engaged to Emma merely cemented what I had already planned in my head.

Yet there was a change. In the run up to our wedding, we've still had our occasional rows. But this time after each row, it never even occurs to me that I shouldn't marry Emma.

NOTES

Foreword

1. Source: Office for National Statistics, "Families and Households: 2018", released in 2019.

Introduction

1. Compared with today's new norm where virtually all couples live together before getting married, just 1% had previously lived together among those who married in the late 1950s, 3% of those who married in the 1960s, and 9% of those who married in the early 1970s. Source: Dunnell, K., Family Formation 1976, London: OPCS, 1979.

2. Claims that there have been high rates of "illegitimacy" throughout history have been comprehensively debunked by Professor Rebecca Probert. Official records back to 1845 show that fewer than 5% of births took place outside marriage. Similarly, fewer than 5% of older adults who married prior to 1945, interviewed for the British Household Panel Survey, lived together before they married. See Probert, R. & Callan, S., History and Family: Setting the Records Straight, London: Centre for Social Justice, 2011.

3. Data from the survey Understanding Society suggests that about half of all parents who are cohabiting when their child is born will go on to marry. The latest Office for National Statistics births data (from 2017) shows that 52% per cent of parents were married when their child was born and 32% were cohabiting at the same address. (A further 11% of newborns were born to mother and father who registered separate addresses and 5% per

cent were born to mothers only.) So 52 plus 16 (i.e. 32 divided by 2) equals 68% of today's new parents who will ever marry.

4. This is from our latest analysis for Marriage Foundation of parents of teens not living with both natural parents. Two big household studies both show it was 36% in 2016. That's actually an improvement on five to ten years earlier, because of a big fall in divorce rates. However, behind that, we see no evidence that the less stable cohabiting couples are making similar improvements. See Benson, H. & McKay, S., "Family stability improves as divorce rates fall", Cambridge: Marriage Foundation, 2019. All of our reports can be downloaded free from www.marriagefoundation. org.uk.

5. Our study of teenage mental health was one of the first in the UK to identify family breakdown as the biggest indicator of problems among teens. This was a huge study and our analysis is very robust. Even after taking into account mother's age, education, ethnicity, happiness with her relationship, and initial marital status, not having a father in the house is the biggest indicator of mental health problems among teens. See Benson, H. & McKay, S., "Family breakdown and teenage mental health", Cambridge: Marriage Foundation, 2017.

6. This is from a study we did of 1,783 mothers with teenage children aged either 14 or 15 when they were surveyed in 2009 or 2010, using data from the national survey Understanding Society. The advantage of being married before your child is born does not appear to apply to those who marry after their child is born. I discuss this slightly unexpected phenomenon towards the end of chapter 7. As a clue, think about whether couples marry because they want to do it or because their families want them to do it. See Benson, H., "Get married BEFORE you have children", Cambridge: Marriage Foundation, 2015.

Chapter 1

1. The comment was made by the character of Anita Olesky in the film *Never Been Kissed*, 20th Century Fox, 1999.

2. This is taken from my updated analysis of a survey of 2,000 UK adults conducted in December 2012 for the law firm Seddons, in collaboration with Marriage Foundation. Of these, 520 women and 345 men were either single, cohabiting, or in a non-cohabiting relationship, but not separated, divorced, or widowed. Among those aged 25–30, 72% of the unmarried women said they wanted to get married, compared with only 48% of the unmarried men. Only 12% of the women rejected marriage outright compared with 28% of the men. Among those aged 31–40, the gender difference was reversed with 57% of the unmarried men wanting to marry compared with 51% of the unmarried women; only 19% of the men rejected marriage outright compared with 26% of the women. More details of this analysis are available from www.marriagefoundation.org.uk.

Chapter 2

1. Weigel, D. & Ballard-Reisch, D., "Investigating the behavioral indicators of relational commitment", Journal of Social and Personal Relationships, 19, 2002, pp. 403–423.

2. Whereas this book is about how we form successful relationships and how we commit to one another, my previous book, co-written with Kate, is about how to make sure our relationship works the best it can. We tell the story of how our own marriage got into an appalling and unnecessary mess soon after the birth of our first two children, and how we then resolved it to make our marriage better than ever. Our story is extremely typical of so many parents' experience of drifting apart. If you haven't already read it, I hope you'll find it enjoyable and filled with practical

hope. See Benson, H. & Benson, K., What Mums Want and Dads Need to Know, Oxford: Lion Hudson, 2017.

3. This is the first foundational paper on commitment by Scott Stanley and Howard Markman, before Galena Rhoades (née Kline) came on the scene. See Stanley, S. & Markman, H., "Assessing commitment in personal relationships", Journal of Marriage and Family, 1992, pp. 595–608.

4. If you wanted to venture at all into the academic research on commitment, this would be the paper I'd suggest you start with. It's a fairly easy read and covers the subject really well. There are free pdf copies on the web if you google. See Stanley, S., Rhoades, G., & Markman, H., "Sliding versus deciding: Inertia and the premarital cohabitation effect", Family Relations, 55, 2006, pp. 499–509.

5. Stanley, S., Rhoades, G., & Whitton, S., "Commitment: Functions, Formation, and the Securing of Romantic Attachment", Journal of Family Theory & Review, 2, 2010, pp. 243–57.

6. Rhoades, G., Stanley, S., & Markman, H., "Should I stay or should I go? Predicting dating relationship stability from four aspects of commitment", Journal of Family Psychology, 24, 2010, p. 543.

7. Using the same survey of young adults – though this time the 1,294 who completed the original survey – Kayla Knopp and colleagues found that constraints felt positive or negative depending on how dedicated they were as a couple. When dedication was low and constraints high, there were signs of increased anxiety and fear of abandonment. But by far the biggest effect was on feeling trapped. Knopp, K., Rhoades, G., Stanley, S., & Markman, H., "Stuck on you: How dedication moderates the way constraints feel", Journal of Social and Personal Relationships, 32, 2015, pp. 119–37.

8. Here are two studies showing that whether or not couples move in before engagement is more important than whether or not they move in before marriage. See Kline, G., et al., "Timing

is everything: Pre-engagement cohabitation and increased risk for poor marital outcomes", Journal of Family Psychology, 18, 2004, p. 311, and Rhoades, G., Stanley, S. & Markman, H., "Pre-engagement cohabitation and gender asymmetry in marital commitment", Journal of Family Psychology, 20, 2006, pp. 553–60.

9. Whether the mere act of living together reduces the chances of having a successful subsequent marriage is the subject of a hotly debated academic discussion. Previous studies have claimed the apparent disadvantage is because some couples move in when they are too young. The most recent study disputes this finding and suggests cohabitation at any age leads to an increased risk of subsequent marital problems. Either way, moving in at a young age is bad news for your prospects. See Kuperberg, A., "Age at coresidence, premarital cohabitation, and marriage dissolution: 1985–2009", Journal of Marriage and Family, 76, 2014, pp. 352–69, and Rosenfeld, M. & Roesler, K., "Cohabitation Experience and Cohabitation's Association with Marital Dissolution", Journal of Marriage and Family, 81, 2019, pp. 42–58.

Chapter 3

1. The key principles of 'deciding, sliding, and inertia' were identified by Scott Stanley and his team at the University of Denver. As mentioned in a previous note, if you wanted to read just one academic paper on commitment, this should be it. See Stanley, S., Rhoades, G. & Markman, H., "Sliding versus deciding: Inertia and the premarital cohabitation effect", Family Relations, 55, 2006, pp. 499–509.

2. In our book What Mums Want and Dads Need to Know, we discuss a well-known review of 100 studies that found only two main areas where men and women differ in any meaningful way: in strength and size where there is little overlap; and in sex-stereotyped activities, such as playing golf (predominantly male) or watching TV chat shows (predominantly female). See

Carothers, B. & Reis, H., "Men and women are from Earth: examining the latent structure of gender", Journal of Personality and Social Psychology, 104, 2013, p. 385.

3. Stanley, S., Whitton, S., & Markman, H., "Maybe I do: Interpersonal commitment and premarital or nonmarital cohabitation", Journal of Family Issues, 25, 2004, pp. 496–519.

4. This study is under her maiden name. See Kline, G., et al., "Timing is everything: Pre-engagement cohabitation and increased risk for poor marital outcomes", Journal of Family Psychology, 18, 2004, p. 311.

5. Rhoades, G., Stanley, S., & Markman, H., "Pre-engagement cohabitation and gender asymmetry in marital commitment", Journal of Family Psychology, 20, 2006, p. 553.

6. It needs to be acknowledged that not all studies find this gender effect when comparing cohabitation history to see how well couples do once married. In another study of 1,000 people married for an average of six years, Galena and colleagues found that the effect of living together before engagement was still negative but smaller than previously found, and no different for men or women. However, she acknowledges that the study design excluded couples who had already divorced, where the gender effect might have shown up most. See Rhoades, G., Stanley, S., & Markman, H., "The pre-engagement cohabitation effect: A replication and extension of previous findings", Journal of Family Psychology, 23, 2009, p. 107.

7. Rhoades, G., Stanley, S., & Markman, H., "A longitudinal investigation of commitment dynamics in cohabiting relationships", Journal of Family Issues, 33, 2012, pp. 369–90.

8. Manning, W. & Smock, P., "Measuring and modeling cohabitation: New perspectives from qualitative data", Journal of Marriage and Family, 67, 2005, pp. 989–1002.

9. Benson, H. & McKay, S., "Family planning", Cambridge: Marriage Foundation, 2018.

10. Bingham, J., "Couples who get a kitten before a baby 'more likely to last'", *The Telegraph*, 15 February 2013.

11. Schippers, M., Scheepers, A., & Peterson, J., "A scalable goal-setting intervention closes both the gender and ethnic minority achievement gap", *Palgrave Communications*, 1, 2015, Article 15014.

Chapter 4

1. This was from a survey of 5,000 adults in England and Wales conducted by YouGov in 2016. Marjoribanks, D. & Bradley, A., *It takes two: Couple relationships in the UK*, Doncaster: Relate, 2017.

2. From the numbers Relate report, I can extrapolate that about two thirds of their sample was married – which is somewhat lower than the national average for couples of 80%. Nonetheless, if worries about commitment are assumed to be spread evenly among men and women in the married group, then unmarried women would be 50% more likely to worry than unmarried men. I asked Relate if we could have a look at their underlying data. Although very helpful, alas they were unable to supply this.

3. For a fuller list, see Stanley, S., et al., "Unequally into 'Us': Characteristics of Individuals in Asymmetrically Committed Relationships", *Family Process*, Vol. 58, 2018. At the time of writing there is a free online version available.

4. For a fuller list, see Stanley, S., et al., "Unequally into 'Us': Characteristics of Individuals in Asymmetrically Committed Relationships", *Family Process*, Vol. 58, 2018.

5. This is another finding from the larger sample of young unmarried adults. See Rhoades, G. & Stanley, S., *Before "I Do": What Do Premarital Experiences Have to Do with Marital Quality Among Today's Young Adults?*, National Marriage Project, University of Virginia, 2014.

NOTES

Chapter 5

1. Stanley, S., Markman, H., & Whitton, S., "Communication, conflict, and commitment: Insights on the foundations of relationship success from a national survey", *Family Process*, 41, 2002, pp. 659–75.

2. Fincham, F., Beach, S., & Davila, J., "Forgiveness and conflict resolution in marriage", *Journal of Family Psychology*, 18, 2004, pp. 72–81. Also Fincham, F., Beach, S., & Davila, J., "Longitudinal relations between forgiveness and conflict resolution in marriage", *Journal of Family Psychology*, 21, 2007, p. 542.

3. Modern research findings mirror ancient biblical advice on gender distinctions. Husbands are told to "love your wives, just as Christ loved the church and gave himself up for her" (Ephesians 5:25). That's a big statement about men in particular being willing to sacrifice. Husbands are also to "love your wives and do not be harsh with them" (Colossians 3:19) and treat them "in an understanding way, showing honour" (1 Peter 3:7, ESV). This shows the importance of treating women well. Equally there are important warnings to beware the way some women handle conflict. "Better to live on a corner of the roof than share a house with a quarrelsome wife" (Proverbs 21:9 and 25:24). There are three other similar warnings in Proverbs 19:13, 21:19, and 27:15. However choose wisely and the rewards are huge: "A wife of noble character who can find? She is worth far more than rubies" (Proverbs 31:10–11).

4. Whitton, S. et al., "If I help my partner, will it hurt me? Perceptions of sacrifice in romantic relationships", *Journal of Social and Clinical Psychology*, 26, 2007, pp. 64–91.

5. Stanley, S. et al., "Sacrifice as a predictor of marital outcomes", *Family Process*, 45, 2006, pp. 289–303.

6. Whitton S. et al., "If I help my partner, will it hurt me? Perceptions of sacrifice in romantic relationships", *Journal of Social and Clinical Psychology*, 26, 2007, pp. 64–91.

7. Owen, J., Rhoades, G., & Stanley, S., "Sliding versus deciding in relationships: Associations with relationship quality, commitment, and infidelity", *Journal of Couple & Relationship Therapy*, 12, 2013, pp. 135–49.

Chapter 6

1. The bad habit of reacting negatively during conflict tends to predict divorce in the early years, but not the later years. In contrast, the good habit of reacting positively during both conflict and everyday discussions tends to predict divorce in the later years, but not the early years. Gottman, J. & Levenson, R., "The timing of divorce: Predicting when a couple will divorce over a fourteen-year period", *Journal of Marriage and Family* 62, 2000, pp. 737–45.

2. This is from a detailed study of how 100 couples actually argued, based on a daily diary they were asked to complete in real time over a two-week period. See Papp, L., Cummings, E., & Goeke-Morey, M., "For richer, for poorer: Money as a topic of marital conflict in the home", *Family Relations*, 58, 2009, pp. 91–103.

3. Four of the most negative behaviours have variously been labelled The Four Horsemen. This is a tumbling cascade of negativity where Criticism turns into Defensiveness, which then creates Contempt, and eventually Stonewalling. See Gottman, J., *What Predicts Divorce?* Hillsdale, NJ: Erlbaum, 1994. Another group sees them as individual Danger Signs, which are Escalation, Negative Interpretation, Invalidation, and Withdrawal. See Markman, H., Stanley, S., & Blumberg, S., *Fighting for Your Marriage: A Deluxe Revised Edition of the Classic Best-seller for Enhancing Marriage and Preventing Divorce*, John Wiley & Sons, 2010.

4. Lion Hudson, 2013.

5. Studies of attribution have been around for a long time, pioneered by Professor Frank Fincham, currently at Florida State University. These show a strong link between the way couples attribute behaviour and how satisfied they are in their marriage. In this study, he demonstrated that attribution influences marriage, and not vice versa. Fincham, F., Harold, G., & Gano-Phillips, S., "The longitudinal association between attributions and marital satisfaction: Direction of effects and role of efficacy expectations", *Journal of Family Psychology* 14, 2000, pp. 267–85. More recent enquires have shown that attributions are most likely borne out of attachment insecurity. Kimmes, J., et al., "The role of pessimistic attributions in the association between anxious attachment and relationship satisfaction", *Family Relations*, 64, 2015, pp. 547–62.

6. This is the extraordinary counter-intuitive finding that every parent considering splitting up should know about. Children are often better off out of a high-conflict relationship. But the end of a low-conflict relationship is simply confusing. It makes no sense to them. See Booth, A. & Amato, P., "Parental pre-divorce relations and offspring post-divorce well-being", *Journal of Marriage and Family*, 63, 2001, pp. 197–212.

Chapter 7

1. See Benson, H., "Get married BEFORE you have children", Cambridge: Marriage Foundation, 2015.

2. Benson, H., "Get married BEFORE you have children", Cambridge: Marriage Foundation, 2015.

3. In our studies of the millennium children when they were aged eleven, marriage usually came out as the top indicator of whether parents stayed together. But in our most recent studies of the same children at age fourteen, we found that mother's happiness with

the relationship soon after the baby was born and mother's age came top, followed by whether she was married, and then whether she had a degree, whether the birth was planned, and finally mother's religion and ethnic origin. Of course, happiness and marriage are related anyway, whether because those who marry become happier in their relationship or the other way round. See Benson, H. & McKay, S., "Family Planning", Cambridge: Marriage Foundation, 2018.

4. Teenage mental health is hugely dependent on the family environment. Our first analysis of teenage mental health, again looking at the fourteen-year-olds in the Millennium Cohort Study, showed that the single biggest risk factor was whether the child's father was also living in the house or not. Family breakdown was the top factor for girls and equal top factor for boys, along with how happy the mother was when the child was born. Our study took into account the parents' marital status, age, education, and ethnicity. See Benson, H. & McKay, S., "Family breakdown and teenage mental health", Cambridge: Marriage Foundation, 2017.

5. Francis-Tan, A., & Mialon, H., "'A Diamond Is Forever' and Other Fairy Tales: The Relationship Between Wedding Expenses and Marriage Duration", *Economic Inquiry*, 53, 2015, pp. 1919–30.

6. Rhoades, G., & Stanley, S., "Before 'I Do': What Do Premarital Experiences Have to Do with Marital Quality Among Today's Young Adults?", National Marriage Project, University of Virginia, 2014.

7. Benson, H. & McKay, S., "Family planning", Cambridge: Marriage Foundation, 2018.

8. Benson, H., "Men behaving well", Cambridge: Marriage Foundation, 2019.

Chapter 8

1. Slovic, P. & Corrigan, B., "Behavioral Problems of Adhering to a Decision Policy", paper presented at the Institute for Quantitative Research in Finance, Napa California, 1973.

2. Tsai, C., Klayman, J., & Hastie, R., "Effects of amount of information on judgment accuracy and confidence", *Organizational Behavior and Human Decision Processes*, 107, 2008, pp. 97–105.

3. Heath, C., & Gonzalez, R., "Interaction with others increases decision confidence but not decision quality: Evidence against information collection views of interactive decision making", *Organizational Behavior and Human Decision Processes*, 61, 1995, pp. 305–26.